Wild Crone Wisdom

Poetry and Stories

Edited by
Stacy Russo and Julie Artman

Wild Librarian Press
Santa Ana, California

Library of Congress Control Number: 2023910954
Paperback ISBN: 978-1-7376759-3-8
E-book ISBN: 978-1-7376759-4-5

Cover and interior book design by Sarah E. Holroyd
    (https://sleepingcatbooks.com)
Cover art "Anna" by Charlotte Hildebrand

Published by Wild Librarian Press, Santa Ana, California

www.wildlibrarianpress.com

Wild Librarian Press
Santa Ana, California

Thank you for supporting a woman-owned independent press!

Contents

3   Introduction
STACY RUSSO

CREATIVE NONFICTION

9   Loss as Gain
KARINE HALPERN

13   Lifeline
ANNE HOFLAND

18   Nana Tries to Get Me in the Shower
D. D. WOOD

24   True for Today
ELLEN SHRINER

29   The In-Between
J.T. MARLOWE

31   The Value of Dog Weight
HILLORIE SUE MCLARTY

35   La Danse Macabre: On Starting Ballet Lessons at 70
ELIZABETH KENNEDAY

40   Salsa
RITA WILSON

44   The Gift of a Hug
NANCY KING

47   Growing Old the Alice Way
LYNN MARTIN

49   Be Happy – and Keep Your Mouth Shut
MARGARET M. RODEHEAVER

52   Permanent Ink
JOANN BREN GUERNSEY

Nonfiction

58   Silver Singles Dating Bio
      Penelope Page

Short Stories

63   Fear of Emptiness
      Indra Chopra

68   Something Personal
      Miriam Karmel

71   Attraction
      Caryn Coyle

76   A Sunday Intrusion
      Nancy Werking Poling

80   Confession
      Lenore Hirsch

Poetry

87   Organs
      Stella Brice

88   SOAR Studio
      Suzanne Freeman

90   How Scotch Broom Came to Dallas
      Suzanne Rhodenbaugh

92   Arlee
      Suzanne Rhodenbaugh

94   The Lady of the Garden
      Elaine Namanworth

96   The Second Beauty
      Elaine Namanworth

98   Spinster
      Claudette Mork Sigg

100   Matriarch in the Garden of Bees
      CLAUDETTE MORK SIGG

102   Garden Walk with the Chairmaker's Wife
      CINDY RINNE

104   Home: Winter Crossroads
      CINDY RINNE

105   What Gathers In
      ANITA PINATTI

106   Deconstructed Soup
      ANITA PINATTI

107   I Still Get Hunger
      SUSAN CAVANAUGH

108   Kitchen Crumbs
      RONNA MAGY

109   Tree
      JEANNE BRYNER

111   Midden
      JEANNE BRYNER

113   The Crone
      ANA MARÍA CARBONELL

114   The Sentence
      ANA MARÍA CARBONELL

117   La Vieja
      MARY VOLMER

119   Parable of the Oak
      MARY VOLMER

121   Stone Age
      JENNIFER L. ABOD

123   Lesbian Crone
      JENNIFER L. ABOD

124   For Carlos
        TERRY A. ALLBRIGHT

125   Cake
        TERRY A. ALLBRIGHT

127   In the Curve
        PHYLLIS CARITO

128   Arise the Woman
        PHYLLIS CARITO

130   What Remains
        CONNIE LEVESQUE

131   Wild Sisters
        CONNIE LEVESQUE

132   Larkspur Trail
        CAROL BARRETT

134   Snowfall
        CAROL BARRETT

136   Passing Through
        JOAN ANNSFIRE

138   Musical Memory
        JOAN ANNSFIRE

140   Near Her Cauldron Where a She-Fox Leaps
        KATHARYN HOWD MACHAN

141   Dorothea's Hands
        KATHARYN HOWD MACHAN

142   Mad for the Moon
        GAY GUARD-CHAMBERLIN

143   Cornucopia
        GAY GUARD-CHAMBERLIN

145   Remains in Our Days
        JUDITH YARROW

146 If Winter Promises
     JUDITH YARROW

147 My Mother's Hair
     KATHLEEN WEDL

148 Before Calling the Coroner
     KATHLEEN WEDL

149 More Time
     ELIZABETH BRULÉ FARRELL

150 Mending
     ELIZABETH BRULÉ FARRELL

151 The Art of Chickens
     JOANNE M. CLARKSON

153 Salt and Silver
     JOANNE M. CLARKSON

154 To My Thirties
     SUSAN MICHELE CORONEL

156 Dear Grief,
     SUSAN MICHELE CORONEL

158 How Do I Look?
     ROSANNE EHRLICH

160 Sistine Skin
     SHIRLEY FESSEL

162 Make Hay While . . .
     D. DINA FRIEDMAN

164 The Trip
     D. DINA FRIEDMAN

165 Hellcat, Witch or Crone
     ERICA KENT

166 when I was just a girl
     KATHLEEN HELLEN

167   This Old Woman
Russ Allison Loar

169   Her Last Day
Russ Allison Loar

172   Legacy
Pam McAllister

173   Cultivating Rough Edges
Pam McAllister

174   Crone
Eileen Moeller

176   The Prayers of The Body
Eileen Moeller

178   The Birthday Fairy
Meredith Trede

179   Last Laughs with The Banger Sisters
Meredith Trede

180   to live
Theresa W. Paulsrud

181   release
Theresa W. Paulsrud

182   Another Year
Marge Piercy

183   It Slowly Closes In
Marge Piercy

184   There's Madness in My Family
Wendy Tigerman

186   Two of a Kind
Wendy Tigerman

188   Awaken
Jo-Ann Vega

190 Limbo
   Nancy Shiffrin

191 A Child is Born
   Nancy Shiffrin

193 The Dark Queen
   Laurence Snydal

194 Mad Meg (after Breughel)
   Laurence Snydal

195 Making Up
   Terri Watrous Berry

196 And Puppy Dog Tails
   Terri Watrous Berry

197 The Other
   Alison Stone

198 For My Aunt, Recovering
   Alison Stone

199 Night Keepers
   Linda Strever

201 I wear scars on the inside
   JC Sulzenko

202 Do-si-do
   JC Sulzenko

204 Grandmother's Button Box
   Eric Machan Howd

205 Of Icons & Other Things
   Bonnilee Kaufman

207 Competition Amongst Old Friends
   Bonnilee Kaufman

209 About the Contributors

229 About the Editors

Introduction

Introduction

STACY RUSSO

I BECAME INTRIGUED BY the archetype of the Crone long before I was close to cronedom or could even be considered a crone-in-training. I was in my late twenties and early thirties when the Crone came into my life through the work of Clarissa Pinkola Estés, specifically her *Women Who Run With the Wolves: Myths and Stories of the Wild Woman Archetype*, which remains the most cherished book of my life, and also the recordings of her live talks captured in the two-volume *Theatre of the Imagination* that I have listened to countless times over the years.

What was it about the Crone that captivated me as a young woman? This question is a complex one. Discovering the answer would take much more than this brief introduction will allow, but I can say that part of the Crone's attraction for me was the reclamation and celebration of a word that has been used in modern times to often harm, vilify, and marginalize old women. Here was also a way to envision old age that embraced complexity, ambiguity, and the wisdom found in the dark and light. This brought joy. Even in my late twenties, while thoroughly enjoying the life of a young woman, I thought to myself, "How wonderful and exciting to think that I may become a Crone one day!"

I embarked on my journey as a woman with a sense of adventure and let go of the fear of aging that sadly plagues many women. As I matured and entered into my middle years, I never desired to lie about or hide my age and turned away from strict definitions of beauty that only idealize youth. At the same time, I did not go to the other extreme and place old women on a pedestal and only see them as good, wise, and beyond reproach. Although much different than the harmful devaluing of old women that makes them invisible, something to fear, or a nuisance, this alternative, idealized version denies women depth, humanity, and individuality.

Estés' work, as well as the interpretations of fairy tales offered in the work of individuals such as Jungian psychoanalysts Marie-Louise von Franz and Marion Woodman, dismantle these false binary notions of an old woman being purely good or evil and offer the beautifully complex and ambiguous Crone. An example of this is found in the Slavic figure of Baba Yaga, one of my most cherished representations of the Crone. In Baba Yaga there is much depth to interpret. This includes the unpredictability of her behavior, since she may be helpful and kind or sinister and deadly; the mysterious meaning of the spinning motion found in both her rotating hut and the mortar she flies through the air in and navigates with a pestle; the forest where she dwells as a liminal space; the meaning of her magical hut on chicken legs; and, ultimately, the transformative possibilities that follow encounters with her. One needs considerable inner strength to encounter and survive Baba Yaga, yet meeting her brings wisdom to those courageous enough to welcome such an engagement. I have spent much time reflecting on this great Forest Witch and her frightening and wonderfully powerful abilities to both create and destroy.

My decades-long love affair with the Crone led to the vision and eventual creation of this anthology you are now about to enjoy: *Wild Crone Wisdom*! After many years as a writer working within the traditional publishing world where I wrote book proposals, pitched ideas to publishers, signed contracts, waited for royalty checks, and experienced some wonderfully good things and some other not-so-good things, I decided it was time to try something new. Why not start my own small press to publish the work of other writers and my work!? Isn't this exactly the kind of thing a Crone would do? In late 2021, from the kitchen table of my small home surrounded by a wild, large garden – my own version of Baba Yaga's hut – Wild Librarian Press was born. *Wild Crone Wisdom* is the second publication from this new adventure.

The vision of this anthology was always one of openness. The call for submissions was for all genders. The door was wide open for all presentations, imaginations, and understandings of the Crone to be considered. Although my journey with the Crone has been tied to my life as a woman, my understanding of gender has been greatly expanded and liberated over the past two decades through the work and activism of the courageous LGBTQIA+ community I continue to learn from and admire. Certain representations of the Crone, such as Baba Yaga, may be seen as feminine, but these archetypes may also be understood and celebrated as androgynous and non-binary. New understandings of gender offer delicious terrains for us to investigate. It is exciting to consider the future of the Crone and how this archetype may evolve and grow in complexity.

Wild Crone Wisdom is a vibrant addition to the genre of Crone Lit, literary works that focus on the exploration of the Crone.

Other works in this genre include Barbara G. Walker's *The Crone: Woman of Age, Wisdom, and Power*; Jean Shinoda Bolen's *Crones Don't Whine: Concentrated Wisdom for Juicy Women*; the annual "Crone Power Issue" of the poetry journal *Gyroscope Review*; Pat B. Allen's fictional *Cronation*; the anthology *Crone Chronicles 20-20: Intimately Inspiring Glimpses into the Lives of Women 52+* edited by Debra L. Gish; and Clarissa Pinkola Estés' work I have already mentioned above and her wonderful and more recent *The Power of the Crone* and *The Dangerous Old Woman*, both with the subtitle *Myths and Stories of the Wise Woman Archetype*. The contributors to *Wild Crone Wisdom* give much for us to enjoy, reflect on, and be inspired by while offering their voices to the growing Crone Lit genre. Long live the Crone!

Creative Nonfiction

Loss as Gain

KARINE HALPERN

BACK THEN LIFE WENT by without much thought. Certainly, there was no mindfulness. For many years we did not need to talk about being mindful or conscious. There was no focus on self-development. Each individual was concerned, at least in Europe, with a recent war (WW II), and the goal was to simply gain freedom and wealth. Until the year 2000, it seemed work was available for anyone who desired it.

There was something strange in how I, as a little girl, received knowledge about being a woman in the 70s and 80s. One of my grandmothers never worked to make money and the other one worked like a dog, surviving the war with a family business and a daughter who would take up the business to continue it. This grandmother was able to provide work for others. I saw her and her daughter working hard. I saw my other grandmother not working at all. Seeing these two sides, I never worried about having a home because both sides of the family had homes and money.

Cars, bank accounts, new clothing, huge refrigerators full of stuff, and various possessions were things I did not give much thought about. Nor did I concern myself with stuffed garages, basements, and attics. I was simply full of freedom and thinking about the future, yet I was also aware of the writer, explorer, and anarchist Alexandra David-Néel. I have always been a fan of David-Néel, who had to negotiate with her husband to not get a divorce. Women could not have a bank account during her time, and the revenues from her transcriptions, translations, and writings had to be managed by men.

David-Néel was born in Saint Mandé, France, at the intersection of Paris and Vincennes. She traveled all over Asia and died in the Alps in Digne-les-Bains in the South of France. I've read all of her literature, studied her life, and felt compelled to find out why she was so interested in philosophy, politics, Buddhism, and Hinduism. What drove her passion toward self-development in the 20s? She was also into mindfulness, having been drawn there through her spiritual life. David-Néel, it turned out, would appear in a moment of synchronicity when I experienced some dramatic changes later in life.

In the 80s, the 90s, and then again in 2005 and 2014, I lost members of my family. I lost homes and relationships. I lost things. I lost love. I lost jobs. I lost security. The pain was so heavy that I could not walk outside further than the corner of the street. One day I walked to the bakery to get bread. There I found a note for a part-time job on the very same street. Such random findings as a job posted on a bakery wall rarely exist these days.

I got the job. I paid the rent. Still, I needed a solution for my situation, because the rent was too much for a single person. My life was miserable. I decided I wanted to feel better and heal. I visited a real estate agency near the Castle of Vincennes, possibly one of the most expensive places in France. I became friends with the broker in my desire to discover how I could become the owner of my own home. How could this be done as a single woman with zero investments and a part-time job? The broker said that he had something for sale under 100.000 Euros. It was a property poised to be purchased by a friend of his. These types of dwellings are generally not advertised. They sell quickly, since wealthy men desire them for investments, but not to live in them.

I encouraged him to sell the property to me. I would use it as my home. I needed it for survival. He called his friend and told him that the place was not for sale anymore. This is how I came to buy my home.

I have no idea how I was able to succeed in putting together a plan for securing the loans for my home. I don't even recall how I got the will and the energy to renovate the entire place, as it was in very bad shape. On the day of the sale, we gathered at an attorney's office. I was alone, representing myself with no family or friends. I signed and walked to the home, which suddenly belonged to me! I was in debt for many years. I was still broke, but I was happy and proud. I had the keys to my own place! I felt that I existed. I cried. And this is where synchronicity comes into play.

Once I was at my home, I turned and noticed a Parisian sign on the property, indicating it as a landmark. Such signs are typically on display for tourists. The sign read that at this very address, number 57, my new home, Alexandra David-Néel was born! I already felt connected to David-Néel through my knowledge of her writings and life, but now I had become the owner of a piece of land where she was born! I felt transformed.

Over the years, I would renovate. I would redesign. I would rent the place and allow a friend to stay with me for free. But life can still be hard for a woman alone. Loneliness makes us do things we should not. I would eventually succumb to ill advice by a foreign cousin offering a job and a new start in another country. I sold my beloved home based on this cousin's advice.

That is when I lost it all again. I not only lost my home, but my job and friends. I lost my faith. I lost things I loved. I lost myself. I experienced how loss creates an emptiness in one's body. Still, in the depths of this loss, I found a way to fill my emptiness with mindfulness. I realized certain polarities may always be with me:

empty and full, yin and yang, here and over there, now and later. I was connected once again to David-Néel through her self-determination and mindfulness.

At this stage in my life, I no longer suffer over what I own or do not own. I now believe the most powerful way to live is by owning myself and my thoughts. My story has become one of resilience. Through loss, I have gained wisdom.

Lifeline

ANNE HOFLAND

I COULD HAVE OVERLOOKED it, my lifeline. Its arrival was innocuous, just one more email in my crowded inbox. A flyer from Toronto's gay community centre advertised an upcoming writing workshop series for older LGBTQ+ writers.

My heart leapt when I opened it. I had been searching for a writing group for months, had attended sessions in different venues, but never found a good fit. So I immediately submitted the online application for the workshop series, and waited.

My 58th year had been one of tumult. It was a year when I questioned everything in my life, past and present. Recently retired, purposeless and adrift, all the buried demons of my childhood were rising up and threatening to overwhelm me. Restless and discontented, I felt trapped in a life of quiet desperation. I walked out on my 27-year marriage, hit bottom and wallowed there for a time, flirted dangerously with insanity and suicide. My life was at a crossroads, and I was in dire need of a compass.

A week later, the workshop facilitator called to interview me. She informed me that I was one of 25 people vying for 12 spots. She explained that she would be following the Amherst Writers and Artists Method for the workshops, then asked me about my writing experience. In my emotionally fragile state, I did not interview well, and was certain that I would not be chosen. Dejected, I went online to research the workshop method, and immediately felt an almost magnetic affinity to it. It is designed to help writers develop their authentic voice, and to provide a safe space for members of marginalized groups to tell their stories.

I have experienced precious few moments of absolute certainty over the course of my life, but this was one of them. Some inner wisdom told me that this process, this group, at this moment, was a crucial step on my journey.

What happened next was completely out of character. I am a very private person, and rarely advocate for myself, or ask for help. But that day I sat down and e-mailed details of my life situation to the facilitator, a total stranger other than our brief interview. I laid myself bare, explained why I thought this process was so important to me at this point in time, took a deep breath, and pressed "Send."

A week later, the facilitator called to tell me that I had been accepted. Two weeks later, I found myself seated at a table in the back room of a branch of the Toronto Public Library, notebook and pen in hand, a dozen fellow members of Toronto's older LGBTQ+ community around me.

Our facilitator gently led us on a journey of self-exploration through writing. At each session, she provided prompts, we all wrote, then we shared our writing aloud if we chose. We listened deeply to one another, and only offered positive feedback. Each week my fellow writers and I held space for one another as we told our stories of love and grief, triumph and despair, marginalization and hope. Each week we trusted a little more, we dug a little deeper, we allowed ourselves a little more vulnerability. Each week I returned to that table, put pen to paper, and wrote myself down. There were nights when I could barely hold myself together, when the tears flowed before, during, or after the workshops. But each week I went, because the writing, the sharing, the listening had such healing power for me.

I wrote to feel, to uncover, to unravel, to understand, to finally have a voice. I had a happy childhood, so the story goes. There are smiling photographs to prove it, at Christmas with my four brothers and sisters around the tree, on my tenth birthday with my new bike, canoeing in Algonquin Park, camping in the Rockies. I remembered very little of my childhood, so I believed the story – all of it – for decades. Until I became aware that not everyone lives in a constant state of anxiety. Until I started to wonder about the occasional bouts of depression that paralyzed me. Until I started to question my fear of authority, of criticism, of social situations, of confined spaces, of being the centre of attention, of being inadequate -- my fear of being. Until the first time I stood up to my father, in my 50's, and the abject terror that I experienced in that moment did not fit the circumstances, nor the adult me. That terror belonged to the little girl of my childhood. That moment opened a window, just a crack, for the first time, onto the real story of my childhood.

Gradually, the words helped me to express emotions I had suppressed, to bring light to the darkness I hadn't dared to look at, childhood abuse that I had survived and then buried deep. I uncovered ugly truths, both about myself and others in my life, faced up to heart-breaking realizations and harsh realities. The words brought clarity, and compassion. Each time that I wrote about an issue, I could leave a tiny piece of it on the page and walk away a bit lighter.

Little by little, all the other forces that had conspired to silence my voice in this world were pushed back too. As a woman in a patriarchal society, I had continued to serve and obey, and rarely expressed an opinion. As an introvert in a society which values extroverts, I had been overlooked and ignored. As a gay woman in the homophobic world of the 1970's, I was not loud and proud. I chose silence to survive, to protect my career as an elementary school teacher in an era when homosexuality and pedophilia were synonymous. The layers of silence were many and deep, but they began to peel away as I wrote.

I found my voice on the page as I never could have done aloud. The words would flow from pen onto paper in a way that they never seemed to flow through the air. When I tried to speak, the words would stick in my throat, or my mind would freeze and the words wouldn't form. But around that table with fellow writers, or alone in a room, the words would flow down my arm and through my pen and tumble out onto the page, unhurried, uncensored, unjudged. And then I could examine them, make sense of them, rearrange them if I chose.

At first I only shared my words within the writing group. Later, I started reading them to my partner. Although we had separated, we continued to communicate. My writing revealed an inner landscape that I had kept locked away from both myself and her. She gave me the time and space that I needed, and into that space I poured all the words that I hadn't been able to say to her before. The words tore down walls that had been erected between us, brick by brick. Then the words built bridges. The words righted wrongs. The words brought forgiveness. The words brought back love, and laughter. The words saved me, and saved my marriage. And so the words changed everything.

That 58th year may have been the most tumultuous, but it was also the most significant of my years on this earth. It was a year of incredible pain, but also of self-discovery, of facing down fears, of speaking truth, of finding a new path.

As I write this, I hear my partner moving about downstairs in the home we have shared for 36 years now, other than that brief hiatus eight years ago. I smile. Although we can still drive each other crazy sometimes, we no longer take for granted this love that we very nearly lost, so we hold it gently, tenderly, we cherish our time together and stop to savor the moments. Nor do I take for granted my emotional health and sanity, to which I clung by a very slender thread during that terrible but life-changing year. That too, I tend carefully, with writing and art, with solitude and time in nature.

What I seek now in my life is to gather a string of pearls, moments of joy and beauty scattered amidst the mundane, each one gathered lovingly as I spot its smooth polished surface, its iridescent gleam. I want to lift my head from the to-do lists to cherish shared moments with my love, to gaze around me and admire the perfection of nature -- the curl of a wave, the aerobatics of a hummingbird, the sweet scent of pine needles. I want to believe now that the challenges I face are merely opportunities for growth, the universe's way of introducing grains of sand into an oyster shell so that the pearl may form around it. That way, I too may become smoother, more polished -- perhaps even, dare I hope, a tiny bit iridescent.

Nana Tries to Get Me in the Shower

D. D. Wood

I HAD LIVED WITH my mother for many years. First out of necessity and later by choice. Most of the time, we got along fine but every once in a while, *we'd get into it.*

Maybe it was when I was trying to leave for work in the morning and she would decide that it was imperative to tell me a story about when she once "stepped on a small animal and didn't like it." Or when she asked me for the millionth time to show her which button turns on the cable, so that she could blast *Two and a Half Men* re-runs all day long. Or when I was just about to nod off to sleep and I'd hear her Tell-Tale Heart cane thumping down our hallway before she'd shout, "*DeeeeeeDreeeeeee? Are you awake? I said, DeeeeeeDreeeeee, wake up! I need you to look at this mole. It's suspicious.*"

In those moments, I often fantasized about rolling the old woman right out the front door. But I loved her.

Loved her fiercely.

She was the keeper of all my memories, my verbal sparring partner, my literary foil, and I dealt with her quirks and foibles as much as she had always dealt with mine.

It was after her second knee surgery when we had one of our legendary falling-outs. She hadn't bathed in over a week and was ripe in a way that only an old person can be. I suggested that it might be a good idea to wash up a bit.

"Well," she countered. "I've been using these wet wipes they gave me at the hospital." She waved them at me as if I couldn't possibly see them laying on the table next to her. She then threw them back down, disgusted with my lack of hospital hygiene knowledge, and became engrossed in a quick newsflash related to Charlie Sheen's latest antics. "That Charlie." She shook her head at the television and looked back at me. "I don't know what he thinks he's doing going at it with those girls."

I tried not to roll my eyes, but it felt like they went on automatic pilot. Everyone knew why Charlie Sheen was going after those girls.

"Mom," I said, trying to direct her attention back to bathing, "*Mom*," I said again a bit louder. She sighed, exasperated, held up the TV remote and pressed the mute button repeatedly, confused each time the sound turned on-and-off, on-and-off.

"I just don't get this remote," she said. "Something must be wrong with it." She pressed the button flamboyantly one too many times and I snatched it from her hand. "You press it one time, Mom." I paused for emphasis after pressing the button. "See? One time." She ignored me and fed one of the Chihuahuas the left-over bits of her breakfast sandwich.

"Don't feed them that, Mom," I said. "It's not good for them." She grabbed another piece of egg sandwich off her plate, stared me down, smirked, and gave the dog a bite of food. I felt my eye twitch. I considered knocking my mom's old blue recliner chair out from under her while shouting, "Look Old Woman! How do you feel about feeding that damn dog now?" But I refrained.

"You have to take a shower," I said. "Fine," she snapped as she snatched the remote from my hand, dropped it on the TV table, and slowly got up from her chair to walk to her room and get her things together. "Can you at least help me shower?"

"Sure, Mom," I said. "Just call me when you're ready."

I went back into my office to catch up on writing. I didn't hear my hall door open, or the cane thump down the wood floor towards the bathroom, or the shower water begin to run, until I heard, "Ready!" from somewhere . . . I paused, unsure if I had heard her correctly. I got up from my computer and opened the office door.

"Mom?"

"Yes! I'm in the bathroom!" she shouted over the blast of the water.

"What are you doing in *my* bathroom?" I asked through the closed door.

"You said you'd help me," she shouted. "It will be easier if I'm in here."

My shower had an eight-inch step-over ledge. My shower had no handrails or grip tape on the floor. My shower had an old white porcelain soap dish attached to the wall that you could hang on to in case of emergency but could snap off at any moment.

No. It would not be easier in my bathroom.

"Mom!" I shouted. "It's not safe."

"Just come in and help me!" she shouted back.

Suddenly the horrible realization of what she meant by helping her with her shower became quite clear. She didn't want me to hand her a towel or give her a robe or clean clothing discreetly from my side of the door, she wanted me there with her the entire time. *Oh God. . . .* I hadn't prepared for this.

I opened the door slowly and found my mom naked, a full-frontal assault, standing there, waiting for me. I tried to divert my eyes from her naked flesh, confronted with my inevitable future. It was like a scene from *Blue Velvet.*

She carefully climbed into the shower, and I steadied her by keeping my hand pressed gently to her back as she grabbed the soap dish on the wall and centered herself beneath the showerhead. "Oh, that's nice," she said as she felt the warm water rinse over her. She began to scrub up with the bar of soap.

I stood, my back pressed against the wall, and listened to her wash. It wasn't really that bad. I could handle doing this every now and then if she needed me to. I smiled, feeling altruistic and impressed with my ability to handle the situation so calmly. And then I heard the bar of soap hit the tile floor.

"Deidre," my mom said. "Can you come pick up this soap for me and wash my back?"

As soon as I heard her use my full formal name, an unknown force pinned me to the wall like a warning not to go in there alone. "*Deeeeee Dreeee*," I heard my mom call again.

I steeled myself like a good offensive player who tries to recover the play after he fumbles. I took a quick step, grabbed the bar of soap from the floor while trying to ignore my mother's naked ass, and began scrubbing her back.

Then I heard her say, "Oh this is ridiculous! Just take off your clothes and get in here with me. It will be so much easier if you just get naked and wash me down. I need help with my butt."

I don't remember much after that. I believe I tossed the soap towards the soap dish and did some type of cha-cha back pedal out of the bathroom waving my hands to erase the words I had just heard and slamming the door behind me.

"What in the hell are you doing?" she shouted after me.

"That's it!" I screamed. "Get your ass washed and get the *hell* out of that shower now!"

I heard my mom humming softly to herself and knew that she had won this battle. The water soon stopped. She dried herself with the towel I'd left hanging on the rod, then asked me to go grab her robe she'd left hanging in her bedroom.

I walked across the house, angrily whispering to myself, furious that I had been *so stupid* as to be the one to sign up to live with mom. I stomped into the room that she had shared with my father for most of my life, and then stopped, staring at the many photographs and mementos: My baby teeth sitting in a small glass cup. A photograph of me smiling, a tooth missing, red jump suit on, doll in one hand. A card I had given her for Mother's Day last year displayed prominently next to her bed. A photograph of both of us together at my college graduation, her arm wrapped proudly around my shoulders. My wedding photo, the birth of my first child and one of my second—my unwillingness to deliver either baby without her in the room forever documented in those photos. I looked closer remembering her soothing touch as she gently stroked my forehead during labor, her hushed voice whispering, *not much longer now. Not much longer. I'm right here,* until my husband snapped that photo of us: her tired eyes, large smile, with my baby in her arms, me exhausted in the hospital bed looking to her, *looking up to her.*

I felt overwhelmed by the passage of the years and what our future would soon hold, as I gently gathered her robe and quietly walked back down the hall.

"Mom?" I said suddenly humbled. "Are you okay?"

"Yes," she said, "I'm clean now. Are you happy?"

I handed her the robe through the crack in the open door. I wanted to tell her, "No, actually. I'm not. I would prefer you to be young again. I would prefer you to live forever. I would prefer to never think of the day when you won't be here to shout at me from inside of a shower to hurry up and get naked and get in there and help you."

But that's not what I said. I said, "I can't believe you wanted me to wash your ass."

She smiled as she picked up her cane, thumped the floor, and hobbled out past me. "Well," she said. "I always washed yours, you little shit."

I smiled. Happy in the moment; *that she was mine and I was hers.* I knew this dance. It was our *I love you,* and it would *always* be this way.

True for Today

ELLEN SHRINER

MOM LEADS THE WAY through Elder Beerman. "The store where old ladies like to shop," she says and laughs. At 93, she is shorter than she was when I trailed her as a little girl. Then I followed her because only she knew where we were going. Now I let her lead, because she walks so slowly I would leave her far behind if I went first.

Her good tan raincoat hangs straight, disguising how rounded and hunchy her shoulders and upper back are. Her khaki pants look a little short, and I glimpse her socks above her nondescript taupe lace-ups. She hates those plain shoes but her feet hurt, so she wears them.

Walking tires her and leaves her a little short of breath. To shorten the distance to Misses she zigzags through the departments, but she's gotten into the spirit of the outing. "I could use a new top. Maybe we'll find something on sale."

When I was growing up, Mom rarely bought something if it wasn't on sale, so we zero in on the clearance racks. She says, "You never know!" making it sound like a merry treasure hunt. Getting a bargain makes any purchase all the sweeter.

Shopping like girlfriends seems like something mothers and daughters do, at least women of my mother's generation did, so on impulse I suggested it during my visit. Since my father died, Mom is often lonely and doesn't have enough to fill her days. At least one of my three siblings visits her every week, but my sister and two brothers focus on trips to the doctor, grocery store, and church. In truth, I am trying to invent a tradition we never had as adults, because I moved to another state when I was 25. This afternoon I hope to recapture the lighthearted spirit of our shopping expeditions when I was young.

From the time I was about 7 and my sister Margo was 5, we often shopped with Mom. We were old enough to behave ourselves but still young enough to want to be in Mom's orbit. The three of us would flit through Misses like hummingbirds, lighting at one rack after another. Clothes swished and hangers clacked as Mom flipped through them.

If we were at the Lion Store, one of Toledo's better department stores, we visited the coffee shop. Mom would order coffee and pie. Margo and I would get Cokes, a treat, since we didn't get soda often. We'd spin our stools in half circles at the counter, pleased to be old enough to participate in the womanly art of shopping.

Often our shopping trips focused on replacing the clothes Margo and I had outgrown. But when I was about 10, Mom needed something dressy for the Firefighters' Credit Union Dinner Dance. She said her one good dress, the one she wore for anniversary dinners and New Year's Eve parties, "had seen better days." Margo and I were eager to be her collaborators—Mom had so few fancy clothes.

For this shopping trip, Mom brought her pointy-toed high heels in a bag, so she could better judge how dresses would look. She selected a fitted black sheath with a boatneck that dipped to a shallow V in the back. On the hanger, it didn't look like much. But when I zipped Mom into the dress and she slipped on her heels, she was transformed from the mother of four, Girl Scout leader, and room mother she was. She looked slender, sophisticated, and as glamorous as Jackie Kennedy.

We accompanied her to the jewelry counter and she settled on a red rhinestone pin and earrings for dramatic effect. When

Margo and I tried to get her to buy a black beaded evening bag, the spell was broken. She gave the bag a wistful look, then shook her head, "It's pretty, but I'd never get much use out of it."

Nothing appeals to Mom at the clearance rack. We slog to a second rack and she flicks through the clothes. Nothing. A third. I shift my weight from foot to foot, waiting for her to move on or pick something. Anything. Shopping was a stupid idea. Mom doesn't have the interest or energy for this outing. My vision of a carefree excursion with her dims.

Eventually she pulls out two aqua tops. One is a floaty gauze blouse with long sleeves—good for Mom, who is always cold in air-conditioned restaurants. The other is a cotton knit top with three-quarter length sleeves. She has several aqua tops at home, but she likes the color, so I don't mention the duplication. I show her an ivory blouse with a pattern of leaves woven in. She shrugs and says OK. She leads the way to the dressing room and I carry the clothes. The floor is littered with threads, tiny brass safety pins, an occasional straight pin, and white plastic clips that look like little hairpins—just like the dressing rooms I recall from girlhood.

We re-enact our old habits. I sit and Mom hands me her coat and purse. She unbuttons her top and I hold it for her. Mom has always been unselfconscious about undressing in front of Margo and me, so I'm nearly as familiar with her body as I am with my own. She has the same moles and stretch marks she's always had. But in the past few years she has lost 10 pounds without meaning to, dropping from 118 to 108. Her chest is bony, and now her breasts don't fill the cups of her bra.

I hand the gauze shirt to her. She pulls in her lips so she won't mark the top with red lipstick, a gesture I recall from childhood. Once it's on, we eye it, assessing the fit. I flash back to myself at 10-going-on-20. Then I confidently discussed the fine points of style with Mom. Now I'm slower to comment.

The gauze blouse is too big. Mom could wear a size 6, but she's convinced she still needs a 10 and past discussions have taught me not to argue. Yet the image of this thin woman in baggy clothes disturbs me, because she has always cared about how she looks. I wonder if choosing 10's is an old habit, or if she's depressed and has lost interest in her appearance. Maybe she's picking loose clothes because they're more comfortable—certainly her prerogative as a 93-year-old.

I suppress my reaction and strive to sound neutral. "What do you think?"

"I don't know." She shrugs. "Let me see the other ones."

She tries on the next two and makes a face in the mirror. "Nothing looks that great." She sounds defeated. Shopping was supposed to be an enjoyable diversion. Instead, she's been reminded of how age has ravaged her body.

I'm also reminded of the passage of time. It's been decades since I was that happy little girl who liked to shop with her mom.

I don't want our outing to end like this. One shopping trip won't make up for the intervening years and all of the missed moments as an adult daughter, but today I hoped I could push back some of her loneliness and we'd have fun together. If possible, she'd also have the pleasure of getting something new she could look forward to wearing. I want my daydream of mother-daughter shopping—just two grown women laughing, comparing items, and encouraging one another to indulge—to be true this once.

"Really?" I say, "I thought the knit one and the ivory one looked nice."

She brightens. "Maybe you're right. I do get tired of wearing the same things."

"I think you should get them. If you want, I'll buy them for you."

"No, no. I'll buy them." She reasserts herself as the mother, the one who makes the purchase decisions. She is proud that she no longer has to scrimp like she did when we were growing up.

We weave our way through the nearly empty store to a clerk two departments away. Mom hands over the two tops along with her Elder Beerman credit card. In a conspiratorial voice she says, "It doesn't matter that they weren't on sale. I've got money."

We walk out slowly, side by side. Each of us is tired by our effort. But we are lighter too, buoyed by love and our time together.

The In-Between

J.T. Marlowe

IT'S NOT SOMETHING I thought about. It's something I think about now. From time to time. Maybe I should have thought about it then. But then what. To never have stepped into possibility?

He was so intent on eating . . . pancakes. That's the first thing I noticed. Leaning over—long dark hair covering his darker eyes. I took a seat. I can't even form the face anymore—only pieces. Those dark—sad eyes. The happy dimple. The fuller lower lip. The point of his nose. He's a crescent moon—not complete. Later, much later . . . my hands strung through his but mine much older. Clasping at a moment out of time or minutes or years.

You trace it back to that first moment—that first moment of possibility—it seems to happen now. You trace it back to that first moment and you realize it wasn't meant to be. How can you hold on so tight to someone and know you're letting them go.

He skated around the edges. Well . . . because he was a skateboarder and a cook. After he finished his pancakes, he arrived at my table to take my order. He cooked me eggs and made me coffee. I could see him in the kitchen with such earnestness, cooking away. Afterwards, I walked out and he suddenly appeared, skateboarding beside me. He liked my red hair and we talked. Instant, fast, urgent. I would pick him up in my truck and he would throw his skateboard in the bed. We would drive and listen to music. I introduced him to the Beatles. He introduced me to the Clash. He was teaching himself to play the guitar and would leave me phone messages of him trying out new riffs. He had a roommate and so did I (a complicated ex-husband)—which left intermittent, crazy motel nights.

The only thing I remember now, most vividly—believe it or not—not the sex, not even those nights in the back of the cafe after everyone else was gone, watching him clean up the kitchen with such ferocity and then us, against a wall. I remember—not even sure how it came up or what I really needed in that moment which he gave to me—I don't even remember what I said or how I said it—I only remember his words to me, above me, faces hot . . . that heat . . .

"You're pretty . . . I know pretty."

Was I just a cliché, post-divorce? Maybe. I recall that we ended, not unexpectedly, but softly—like his temperament. I was leaving for a time to teach somewhere else. I was taking the train across the country and we met up. He had a gift for me—and to this day—I truly do not understand why he would have given this to me—it was a desk lamp—the heaviest lamp you could ever carry on a train. The only thing I remember about this lamp was its ceramic, tiny ladybug resting along the stand.

And so it goes—on to the next. From lambs to lions. More than twenty years later, eating pancakes, alone. Curious and wondering. Perhaps desire and expectation and disappointment have something to do with it now—perhaps not. Finding his obituary online, his features fully crystallize and a sudden passing at 36. He was only 23 when I knew him.

I wish I could still hear his voice or the riffs he strung his fingers through for me. A sweet subterfuge by memory and the in-between. Beyond a delicate ladybug. Not very subtle, is it?

The Value of Dog Weight

HILLORIE SUE MCLARTY

A LOT OF TIME thinking about weight.
  My weight on the scale
  The weight of the world
  The weight of this thing or the other
  The weight of my conscience
  The weight of my personal responsibilities
When I am at rest, at peace in my mind, and I'm at home, there is a persistent weight, the feel of my dog's body against me, that I sometimes don't even acknowledge. This is what I mean when I say dog weight.

Now some people find it annoying, that heavy/not heavy (depending on size) feeling of a breathing, vibrant body not just next to yours, but leaning on you, making sure you're there, making sure you're not leaving. If I get up for a coffee or snack, or to go to the toilet, the dog is alerted and follows. It's that simple for my dog: I am her person and where I go, she goes.

The happiness of dog weight is temporarily forgotten when I step onto a scale to weigh myself. When did my life become happy or sad due to a number on a scale? I can't remember. I just know that when the number is right, and it rarely is these days, I'm happier than I'm supposed to be. I should not judge myself by a number. Yet, there is that number that I need to have and when I don't have it, I'm not happy.

Not so with dog weight. If it's daytime it is constantly in motion, seeking me, soothing me. Dog weight doesn't care if

31

you're wearing sweats or jeans. Just the touch of my body makes my dog happy, no matter the weight.

My happiness is subjective to the news of the day on the television. Now you might say just turn it off, but I find that difficult. My FOMO looms large. I need to KNOW. Why I need to know is complicated since even when I know there's not a thing I can do about it usually. But I need to know. I need to know who's been shot by whom and why. I need to know who's been lying, screaming, making protestations of innocence. I need to know who's been convicted or not convicted.

Not so with my dog, silently sleeping at my side as I watch the news: it's not that she doesn't care, it's that she's unaffected in that innocent way that is pure. I sit in righteous judgment of it all, thinking I can see through all of the cracks. Until that realization – I am the crack in the judgment – this is when I need dog weight most of all.

Sometimes a big decision is headed my way. What to eat for lunch? What to make for dinner? What to wear to class? What shoes to buy? When do I make that phone call? Or should I even make that phone call at all? Should I write my opinion in the comments of my friend's Facebook post? Dare I venture an opinion out loud about something you're doing or not doing? The weight of these decisions pale in comparison to the deeper decisions: should I move to Nashville? Should I borrow the money it takes to get my master's degree at Belmont University? Should I be honest to someone who I've lost trust in? This weighs heavy on me. These are very important decisions and carry a lot of weight.

Not so with my dog, who has travelled these 2,000 miles with a smile on her face and when I'm not flitting around the planet, is so happy just to be near me. This is how dog weight keeps me grounded, keeps me nearer to what I call sane.

Things I have done in the past haunt me to this day. The friend that I lost because I could not keep up. The boyfriend who might have been the best thing ever to happen to me, yet I found boring and wanted the bad boy and more excitement. The day I called in sick too many times to that job and got fired. The day I spoke my mind at work and got reprimanded by Human Resources. The day I sent my mother a mother's day card that said what I really thought: that we'd never had a great relationship so I couldn't just buy her a Hallmark card and be done with it. The day I dropped Gary off at his friend's house not knowing I'd never see him again. The day I had to wear long sleeves to my best friend's summer wedding because I had track marks. This is the weight I carry with me and don't even realize how much it means until I sit down to write it all down and it spills out like so much water under the bridge.

Not so with my dog, who patiently waits for me to return when I've gone out. She smiles at me in that way that I cannot explain. Why she is so happy all of the time I don't know. She hasn't had a perfect life. She lived with me in a hotel room, a house for only a year, and the rest of the time in apartments. But she is still joyous as she runs with her stuffed dog in her mouth and does circle eights around me. Every. Single. Day. Because of this and so much more, that dog weight is my stability, my freedom, my serenity, my bond with the universe.

I don't feel weighed down by my humdrum life of keeping house, preparing dinner, doing laundry, and paying bills. Today I consider it a privilege to be able to manage my money. I've even learned QuickBooks. These are things that have eluded me in my past. These things are the weight I have asked for and craved. This is the welcome weight, the thing that keeps me grounded, the good weight.

Dog weight remains the best part of my day. My heart beats with hers. Someone said, "You buy the ticket, and you know that it is a short ride and it's gonna end long before you're ready for it. But you buy the ticket anyway." This is the sad truth about dog weight. This particular dog weight will end far before I'm ready for it. I embrace it as if it will be taken from me in moments. I hang onto the feeling of the love as best I can. Even when I'm working or reading or watching a movie, that weight is there. The best is when I wake up in the morning and she is respectfully at my side, being careful not to wake John or get in between us. This is respectful dog weight that is ingrained in her – the way she acknowledges the human factor in her life.

Not to acknowledge cat weight would be wrong. Cat weight can be comforting too. But when you reach down to pet the giver of the weight, and it's a cat, you might get bitten. This bite is not meant to harm. This bite is meant to say, "I'm here right by you. So back off." In that cat way that they are both aloof and loving, the cat might then move away from you or she might just stay after giving her warning.

These are the times of hard truths around us. These are the times of insecurity and doubt. These are the times we must cling to the best of our earth and embrace it.

My dog weight as well as my cat weight has nursed me through cancer, chemo, death, loneliness, despair, depression, anxiety, and just general sadness about the state of the world. My wish for you is that you have some great weight to rely on.

La Danse Macabre: On Starting Ballet Lessons at 70

Elizabeth Kenneday

For such a tiny video clip online, both in size and length, I was captivated. I watched it several times with the phrase *la danse macabre* reverberating through my mind. That seemed a grim thought as I found the imagery to be so exquisite and elegant. It was reminiscent of noirish Hollywood films from the 1940s in soft focus black-and-white. Angled from the floor, the camera followed a dancer's feet encased in black pointe shoes. Her *en pointe* steps were slow and deliberate, almost walking, in an entrancing pattern. The depth of my reaction caught me by surprise.

I was enchanted by the ballerina mystique as a child—dancers on their tippy toes in fluffy tutus, capped by glittering tiaras. At age eight I began lessons given by a Russian woman in our neighborhood. I was giddy in my required black leotard with pink tights and practice slippers. I don't remember much from those lessons other than being at the barre learning *pliés* while Madame barked "Dosi cow! Dosi cow!" at me. One of the girls in class cattily informed me that she was saying "Don't stick out!" Apparently, my bum was not properly aligned with my rib cage.

Unfortunately, those lessons did not last long as my father was in the military, and we moved a lot. But my obsession with ballet continued. I read the history of ballet and stories of the classic ballets and biographies of the most famous and innovative ballerinas. I was sure I would return to it one day.

In my undergraduate years at university, I managed to take a semester each of ballet and modern dance as electives. I was enthralled by the first professional ballet I attended at that time— the landmark National Ballet of Canada's 1972 production of Tchaikovsky's *The Sleeping Beauty*, choreographed by Rudolf Nureyev, who performed the role of the handsome prince.

I was, of course, aware of Rudolf Nureyev, the dancer who had famously defected to the West from the former Soviet Union in June of 1961. His performances were described as 'electrifying,' so I was thrilled to get sought-after tickets to this ballet production. Of his obsession with *The Sleeping Beauty*, Nureyev said "When I was first learning to dance in Ufa, my ballet master, who had belonged to the Kirov ballet, used to tell me that *The Sleeping Beauty* was the 'ballet of ballets.' And I couldn't wait to try it. It was with the Kirov ballet that I later discovered what a glorious delight it was!"[1]

Nureyev's choreography largely followed that of Marius Petipa, often called "the father of classical ballet" for his accomplishments in choreography in the late nineteenth century, but elaborated the male dancer's role, forever changing the significance of the male performance in classical ballet. Showcasing his own prowess in magnificent leaps and spins during that famous performance, Nureyev had the entire audience, including myself, gasping.

Although I've attended many ballet productions since, the vision of Nureyev's powerful, yet elegant, movements onstage remain clearly in my mind to this day. His dancing was so *alive*! I had never thought of dance that way before, but it left a lasting impression on my thinking about all creative endeavor—that it should be *alive*.

---

1   "Rudolf Nureyev and the Sleeping Beauty," The Rudolf Nureyev Foundation (www.nureyev.org).

While my profession lay in the visual arts, I never stopped longing to develop skills in ballet. I had a brief stint with lessons when I lived near a notable ballet company, but my career led me elsewhere. I tried online lessons with some success when video learning began to proliferate, but I clearly needed a live tutor for corrections if I had any hope of succeeding.

Retiring to Reno, Nevada—a city with a surprisingly lively cultural life beyond the rodeo and casinos—I became aware of the celebrated Sierra Nevada Ballet Company. I also discovered they offered adult ballet lessons but thought, surely, they would consider me beyond the age of such an endeavor. Then I read Director Rosine Bena's assertion regarding ballet and age that "If you can walk, you can dance." That was encouraging as I walk between three and five miles daily.

My age still made me hesitate to pursue it until one evening when my friend and neighbor Francie came to our house for Happy Hour. A bit of serendipity led the conversation to our mutual unrequited obsession with ballet. She had been a dance minor in college, still taking ballet lessons from time to time, including at Sierra Nevada Ballet some years earlier. I took her upstairs to show her my mini studio, and she began jumping and twirling around the room exclaiming we should take lessons together. I caught her enthusiasm immediately but told her I was 70 and wasn't at all sure about the wisdom of such a venture. Ten years younger, she said "Nonsense," called the Sierra Nevada Ballet Company and learned we could join the class the following Tuesday. Which we did.

As we left that Tuesday morning, she surprised me by confessing her nervousness. I told her I was nervous as well, but she shouldn't be as she had so much more experience than me. I worried as well that the established class members might be annoyed by new participants slowing things down—especially me, who hadn't had an in-person lesson since 1985.

The women in the class couldn't have been more welcoming and encouraging. I felt we were off to a good start. As Alex, our Ballet Master, began the initial stretches and pliés, I began to feel hopeful that I might just pull it off. He was very kind, giving badly needed corrections in the gentlest way.

By the time we entered centre work, however, I wondered why I thought I could possibly do this. I knew my muscles would be sore, but my lack of stamina and the slowness of my movements were disconcerting, while Francie was literally leaps and bounds beyond me—the ten-year difference in our ages?

To add to my exertion woes, the extra poundage I'd acquired over the past decade or so made certain movements, such as eight successive *soubresauts* ("sudden" jumps straight up in the air with pointed toes), especially cringeworthy. Light and airy they were not.

Despite my dismay over my physical deficiencies, I was exhilarated on a very profound level. My cherished dream of ballet lessons was finally happening and no one at the company was discouraging me as I feared. I was dogged in my determination to continue to develop strength and speed. I had long harbored a secret desire to dance *en pointe* (gulp!), even at my age.

I researched the topic and found that, yes, it is possible for adults to start pointe work, but it would likely take two years of near daily practice. My physical therapist at the time, a former ballerina herself, was certain I could do it, but cautioned me not to remain *en pointe* for more than fifteen minutes at a time. That was startling as I was thinking I'd be thrilled to dance on my toes for maybe a *pas de bourrée* or two!

Reflecting on the diminutive dance that prompted my thought of *la danse macabre* I had to wonder why it haunted me so. After all, I had seen the astonishing dancing of Rudolf Nureyev in one of the most opulent ballets ever produced, while this dancer's movements were measured and she was devoid of any of the trappings traditionally associated with ballerinas and ballet.

As an artistic motif *la danse macabre*, or the dance of death, originates in medieval times when its plagues and wars decimated the population with alarming regularity. Often depicted by skeletal beings, Death roams alongside the living, often walking in tandem with their earthly counterparts. In an era when the Black Death alone took 25 million people between 1347 and 1352, the message was a reminder that all paths in life will eventually lead to the grave—that death is always near.

Variations of the motif are still wildly popular in contemporary times. For me, that spidery dance became my personal *danse macabre* although I interpreted it in a more uplifting way. I still stumble through some of the more complex combinations and fatigue more quickly than I'd like in my lessons. I get frustrated and discouraged by my seeming lack of progress. I wonder if the effort is all in vain.

Despite those gloomy thoughts, I manage to depart the dance studio feeling inspired to return. I may not have started those long desired ballet lessons until age 70, but I *am* still alive, and I may yet dance on my tippy toes.

Salsa

Rita Wilson

I'M AT A FUNDRAISER for the local chamber of commerce with my husband. It's at a place called Rosalea Farms – someone's estate and barn. It's a perfect summer night. The oppressive humidity that has pressed on the city for the past two weeks has been blown away by the previous night's thunderstorms and left in its wake a perfect sky – the kind with big cumulus clouds and soft breeze. We get out of the limousine which has shuttled us down a long driveway flanked on either side with green fields and tall pines. A man in a light brown suit greets us with peach sangria, and we work our way past pastel linen-covered tables full of items available for bid at the silent auction – coupons for hotel stays, dinners, or dance lessons, and large gift baskets with candles and wine wrapped in cellophane, or cigars and golf balls. We walk over to the large barn, where tables have been set with succulent samples of food from local restaurants for those willing to pay $75 for a ticket or have their companies pay. We help ourselves to red and black tortilla chips with duck confit, and mahi-mahi with coconut rice and mango. We try the Moscato wine, served deliciously cold with its crisp orange and lemon notes. I notice that most of the men have beer bellies, and I comment on it. My husband tells me that he's lost nine pounds, but it's the same nine he keeps losing, then gaining back. The women look nice in their summer dresses and sandals or long flowing tops over straight pants and platform shoes. I compliment a woman on her long dress that looks like it is done in intricate beadwork. Close up, it's just a design.

I like this fundraiser with its bucolic setting. Behind the barn is a fenced-in area with a few white goats, some brown chickens, and a long grey burro. We walk past this field to a guesthouse, which is usually open for public view. We open the door, but inside are a couple of cardboard boxes on the floor in the front room and a man's straw fedora on the table. We quickly close the door and climb back up the hill, my heels sinking slightly into the soft ground. A six-piece salsa band has begun to play in front of a makeshift dance floor. My husband sees a man he knows, and we walk over to his table to say hello to him and his client. We stand around a high-top table covered, as all the others are, with a light rose tablecloth and a glass jar centerpiece containing sand and shells and wrapped with straw on the mouth of the jar. The music stops and the MC announces that they will be giving salsa lessons and encourages the crowd to come up to the dance floor. The three men at the table look at each other. "Come on," I say to my husband. He looks uncertain. The other men laugh.

"Uh, no, that's ok."

"Come on, it'll be fun," I say, and nod toward the dance floor. We had taken lessons for my daughter's wedding and danced a pretty nice rhumba at the reception after about eight weeks of practice. He furrows his eyebrows and shakes his head no. The men look down. "Suit yourself," I say, and put my purse and wine glass on the table. I head to the dance floor without looking back.

About sixteen or seventeen of us congregate on the small floor made of twelve-inch by twelve-inch wood squares that are snapped together. I'm glad that I'm wearing low-heeled black sandals. I'm dressed in a blue-green sweater set and black cigarette pants. I had my blonde hair highlighted in the afternoon, and I'm feeling pretty. The instructor high-fives all of us in a circle, then has us form three lines, all facing the stage, and he goes over the basic salsa step. He has us count one-two-three-four-five-six as we move first forward, then back. Then we put a little rhythm into it. "ONE – two three, FOUR – five six," "SLOW – quick quick – SLOW – quick quick." I notice the tall, brown-skinned man next to me, or rather I feel his presence. The instructor shows us how to move side to side and tells us to put our hips into this. The man next to me is getting closer with each side-to-side movement. He is wearing sunglasses and a close beard, and his mouth is full and wide. I notice that he is wearing a striped long-sleeved shirt and jeans and light teal suede loafers. He pulls this off, somehow. The instructor stops the music, and the man leaves the dance floor. I'm disappointed to see him go, but I turn my attention to the instructor, who now has us line up across from each other – men across from women. There are only six men, and about ten women. The instructor steps in, and one of the women moves across to the men's line. The man in the teal shoes comes back and gets into line directly across from me. "I have my partner," he says. He smiles and points to me, and I smile back. The instructor explains how the women will have to start backwards for this to work and has us practice apart from each other. Then he tells us to join hands. My partner is holding a bottle of beer in his right hand, and he takes my right hand loosely with his left. He introduces himself as Lee. "Rita," I say. The music plays a slow salsa rhythm, and we begin to dance. Forward, back, side to side. He sets down his beer and takes my hands. We all follow the instructor's commands, and then Lee and I break formation and he twirls me around the dance floor.

"You've done this!" I say.

"I'm Latin," he explains, and I try to follow his lead, but he is far better than I am at this. The instructor pauses the music and asks everyone to get back into line.

"Uh oh, we're in trouble," Lee says. We dance to another Latin song which I do not recognize, but Lee does, and he begins to sing and spin me around.

"My husband is going to have a fit," I say.

"Because you're dancing with me?"

"His loss," I say.

The lesson finishes and we applaud. Lee takes my hand. "I enjoyed dancing with you. I hope to see you again."

I walk back to the table where my husband is now standing alone. He does not have a fit. But he doesn't say anything, either. "Where are your friends?" I ask. He shrugs. I take a sip of my wine.

"I saw you out there," he says.

I have no reply.

"Nobody else was doing what you were."

"Nope, they weren't," I say, and pause. "You should have come with me."

"I know," he says. I wonder if he is aware of the difference between knowing and *knowing*.

The Gift of a Hug

NANCY KING

I'M ALMOST EIGHTY-SIX, HIKING mostly alone since the pandemic began. Friends aren't too happy about my solo mountain trips but the alternative of not hiking is unacceptable. From the time I was old enough to understand anything about depression, I learned that being active outdoors helped me feel better, helped calm my nervous system, helped center me. I'm lucky. Living in Santa Fe means easy access to wonderful mountain hikes. So, I hike. Three times a week. Grateful.

On a lovely spring morning, I was hiking down a steep trail, lost in thought. Somehow the past had become present. Annoyed at myself for only remembering bad times, I forced myself to think of something good. In the process, I forgot to look where I was going and tripped on a loose stone, falling headfirst, narrowly missing jagged rocks as I let go of my hiking poles and twisted my body to protect my head. Cursing my carelessness, I surveyed the damage. Blood on my legs and arms showed only surface cuts, easily taken care of. My hip was bruised, but moving my arms, legs, fingers, and toes revealed nothing was broken. I sat for a moment, drank water, took arnica pellets (a homeopathic remedy that helps reduce bruising and swelling), ate a bit of protein bar, and stood up.

My options were to go back up the steep trail and hike for two and a half miles or keep going down the steep trail and hike the four and a half miles to the trailhead. I decided to keep going, focusing on the trail, watching for loose stones, sending energy to the hurting parts of my body.

Suddenly I stopped. A woman was watching me, a smile on her face. Her dog, a collie, I think, sitting quietly beside her, looking at me, its tail swishing back and forth. Embarrassed, I apologized. "I'm sorry. I didn't see you. Sometimes when I'm hiking I forget to pay attention to where I am."

"No problem," she said. Maybe it was her tone of voice, or mine, but the dog got up and gently pressed its body against me, tail wagging. I stroked the thick fur, its tail swishing even faster. This is not the first time a dog on a trail has nuzzled me, but her dog seemed to really want my attention. The woman smiled. "My dog obviously likes you. Is it okay that she's snuggling you?"

"It's more than okay. It feels great. I had to help my cat die a couple of months ago and I miss her cuddling."

We talked for a few minutes about her dog and my cat. We both lived alone and depended on our animals for hugs and cuddles.

"Are you getting another cat?" she asked.

"I don't know. Mia lived seventeen months beyond what the vets thought she'd live, and the last five or six months were pretty difficult. I'm not ready to take care of another cat, but it's hard living without her snuggles, particularly at night. She used to drape herself around my head after I turned out the light. Sometimes her paw would rest gently on my cheek." I could feel myself tearing up. The dog continued to nuzzle me.

"I think my dog knows you miss your cat," she grinned.

"Fine with me," I nodded, grateful for the woman's caring. Usually when I meet people on the trail with their dogs, we say hello and continue hiking. She seemed in no hurry, perfectly happy to share her dog with me.

"You need a hug?" she asked.

"I do," I admitted, more than a little startled by the unexpected question.

She moved toward me just as I moved toward her. We hugged. Two women on a trail, her dog caressing us both. A soft landing after a hard fall.

Growing Old the Alice Way

LYNN MARTIN

WHEN I THINK ABOUT growing older, I think of someone like Alice. Alice was one of my mentors. She was from Putney, Vermont. I didn't meet Alice until she was well into her eighties. Almost everyone knew Alice. She belonged to the Society of Friends, both literally and metaphorically. It had been arranged for me to visit Alice one winter afternoon and read my poetry to her. I found her in the kitchen of an old farmhouse. A big, old-fashioned, plenty-of-room-to-can-hundreds-of-green-beans kind of kitchen. Alice was sitting in a stuffed armchair way off in the corner by the wood stove. Next to her was a small table with a radio on it. At her feet, by her side, under the chair, crowding the radio were books, books, books: biographies, poetry, geographies, histories, and Gore Vidal. "I probably shouldn't like him," she said with a mischievous smile. "He didn't like women very much, but, oh, he can write."

Alice had a hearing problem. "Pull that kitchen chair over here," she commanded, "and sit real close." I removed a bright blue beret off the chair and dutifully put it where she pointed. I didn't know at the time this was her trademark. Alice wore it everywhere. From under it, she moved through town with the concentrated verve of a British packet boat bringing the long awaited news to a knowledge-starved outpost. So, I sat not a foot away, looking directly into her eyes. I read a poem. She listened

47

intently, her lips moving soundlessly, her whole body drinking in the sound. When I finished, we sat in silence. Then she picked up the theme of what I had said and wandered off with it. She crisscrossed the air with reminiscences, tales of Central America, certain plants in her garden, memories of her mother and father, stories of early civil rights battles. She took my poem and, as I sat there, it grew up, matured, encompassed the world. And again, we were silent, until I began to read another poem.

Those few hours with Alice Holway were enchanted. The ultimate poetry reading of my life. The kitchen faded away around us. Blue herons flapped their wings. Off in the distance an owl hooted. Many languages hummed in my ear. I could have stayed there forever.

Alice is no longer with us. I have her picture glued to the wall over my desk. Some days are full of stress. The pace of life seems to be stuck on hurry. When I am crazy with grief or exhausted with loss, I look at Alice. She looks at me from under her beret. The silence settles on my shoulders. I take a deep breath and inhale her calm voice. There is more than this minute, I tell myself. There is, you know, love.

Be Happy - and Keep Your Mouth Shut

MARGARET M. RODEHEAVER

I RECENTLY MOVED INTO a beautiful new house. Well, not actually new, but new to me. And I'm thrilled with it. So why can't everyone be happy for me?

Ever since my husband Pat and I bought the house, other people can't stop pointing out what's wrong with it, and telling me how miserable I'll be in it.

I guess the move took them by surprise. When I browsed through a real-estate magazine in a restaurant lobby one evening, it could have been just an idle pastime if we hadn't already thought about moving. There was really nothing wrong with our old house – but actually everything was wrong with it.

For one thing, both of us had retired. And who needs a house in a part of town where neither of us works anymore?

The yard work and landscaping were more than we wanted to maintain. You probably can't imagine how many hundreds of pine cones I used to pick up and put in the trash each week.

There was a swimming pool in the back yard that we barely used. In fact, Pat routinely threatened to fill it in.

The biggest problem of all was that the house had two stories. If we were downstairs, whatever we needed was upstairs, and vice versa. Between my knees and Pat's bifocals, the stairs were becoming a hazard. Top that off with the fact that a neighbor of ours actually died after a fall down his own stairs, and we had all the reasons we needed to seriously consider moving.

Apparently it was meant to be. After less than a month of house-hunting we made an offer, and soon after that we had a buyer for our old house.

The new house is everything we were looking for. It's all on one floor. The surrounding yard has simpler landscaping and no swimming pool. And it's in a part of town that's closer to relatives and more convenient to the activities we enjoy.

So what's the problem?

I just wish everyone else would be as delighted as I am. But friends and relatives keep finding fault with our new house. I've changed the names below, although I'm not sure why.

Before actually moving in we showed the house to "Maria," our friend and former cleaning lady. The first thing she noticed was how much smaller it is, and how much less storage space there is. It's called *downsizing*, Maria – something people are encouraged to do at our time of life.

Maria also found fault with the new bedroom furniture. Personally I think everyone deserves a new bedroom set after thirty five years of marriage. But Maria thought our new furniture was too dark, and would show the dust too readily.

Cousin "Delores" admired our new house while I was within earshot, but to my husband she confided a different story.

Remember, our new house is all on one floor. It's built on a slab so there are no stairs. Delores lamented how the floors would be our undoing. She groaned about what agony it was when she worked at a business with a concrete floor.

Poor Delores has been unhappy with her own house for a long time. She wants to either redecorate, move, or burn the house to the ground, but she can't get over her own indecision and inertia to do anything. I think she's actually just jealous. Eat your heart out, Delores.

The person who surprised me the most was my 90-year-old

mother-in-law. I thought she'd be thrilled that her number-one son was moving to a house just a mile and a half from hers. And she is happy about that. But she had dire warnings for us, nevertheless.

"You're going to be sorry you moved into such a small house."

"With all the heat vents in the ceiling, your feet will freeze in the winter."

"You're going to hate it when you have to drive all the way back to [previous town] to do your shopping or go to a restaurant."

Sigh. Is it just that people have no filters, and say whatever pops into their head? Maybe their mothers never told them, "If you can't say something nice, don't say anything at all."

I can only imagine what they would say if I'd brought home a new baby:

"Gosh, that thing is shaped funny."

"Wouldn't you rather have a bigger baby?"

"You're going to be sorry when it keeps you up all night."

"Babies are so hard to keep clean."

I love my new house. It's everything I wanted. So just be happy – and keep your mouth shut!

Permanent Ink

JoAnn Bren Guernsey

IT MAY NOT BE so unusual nowadays but, yes, kids — I do have a tattoo. On my butt. Your fat and frumpy grandma is no longer willing to lower her drawers enough for you to see the blue flower hidden underneath. But in my 40s I was all too happy to expose my body, gleeful in my sexuality and daring. My tattoo was a way to announce who I'd become: a previously innocent Midwestern farm girl, almost Kafkaesque in my transformation into a trollop, or at least a Bohemian true to my Czech heritage. Or maybe it was more about my coming of age in the Sixties, the flamboyant Woodstock era — a flower child, a make-love-not-war girl, leaving all underwear at home to dance and sing in fields and let the sunshine in.

To be honest, though, it was mostly because of your Grandpa Andy, my favorite "bad boy" for over 30 years now. He bought the tattoo for me as a birthday gift. We were less than a decade into our love affair, which was no longer illicit but gaining steam nonetheless. I recall a day he doodled on me with a blue marker, and I asked him to do an actual tattoo — with a needle wrapped in thread and dipped in India ink. After all, he'd used this method to permanently inscribe his name (followed by the enigmatic question mark and pair of dice) on his own forearm, back when he was a wild, wayward youth. I reminded him that I had become a wild, wayward woman. But we wisely decided to leave it to a tattoo artist instead. Andy was in the room with me, locating the spot it should occupy on my backside, and watching its application with almost clinical interest. (What they say is true: it hurts like hell!)

Uh oh. You may have just gotten stuck on the word *illicit* because you don't think of our relationship that way, do you? Well, I was a 40+ year old married woman carrying on with a 50+ year old married man, sneaking kisses and clinches, rendezvousing first in a seedy motel straight out of film noir, and then borrowing a friend's serene but cockroach-infested lake cabin. Soon, after our divorces, we didn't bother to hide — making out in our favorite candlelit pizza parlor, skinny-dipping on scorching hot days to make love in the water, even sharing electric touches in front of everybody. Hard for you to imagine now during these days of cribbage, TV binges, and Metamucil, right? But I hope you remember those glorious times we babysat the two of you, hiking and climbing, picnicking and frolicking, piggybacking and "jazz" dancing. Way back in time when you looked up to us both (whose bent and stodgy bodies have each lost two inches), and not down from your adult height and premature wisdom.

Now I'm 73 and my tattoo's color and symbolism have faded. The blue flower has become plumped and pulled a little askew by the aging process, helped along by junk food and booze. I no longer look at it (or any other part of my body) in the mirror, so I forget the flower's there, only reminded at unexpected times, like when my hip surgeon chuckled about it. Tattoos used to be risqué, now they are ubiquitous. My silly attempt to prove myself a rebel is now a cliché that I don't brag about or even mention.

Why now? Is this a kind of swan song?

No, I'm not dying for heaven's sake. But during the pandemic (which is not over, by the way), nobody my age has felt safe. And Grandpa Andy? Well, he has battled cancer twice and, thanks to his dementia, he needs me to be a caregiver more than anything else. His years as a "bad boy" have taken their toll. He made his choices and so did I, when I fell for him despite his being 13 years older, an alcoholic ex-con, longtime smoker, concussed too many times to count. But we're certainly not alone in experiencing a relationship that is ever-evolving. We live comfortably in a senior residence where he struggles through his crossword puzzles and I relax by knitting hats.

After all these years, just about the only thing that is permanent and hanging in there is my tattoo, so that's why the confession now. The hip joint on my right side, deep beneath the blue scribble, is artificial, same as Andy's left one, while those on our opposite hips are getting creakier by the day — not exactly made for robust carnality. And the sad thing is: I don't really care! Maybe I got sex out of my system before menopause. It's strange but true that I've started fast-forwarding through steamy sex scenes in movies. Have I given in to age and cronedom? No, just trying hard to accept and embrace who I have become. We have thousands of photos to share, incredible reminiscences, laughter and tears. Thank god for all of that.

So, kids, I doubt any of this shocks you, and I'm guessing my mention of butts and carnality causes embarrassed giggles even though you are, in fact, adults. But that's okay with me. When you search through my things after I'm gone, you'll find a few nude photos of me and they will make you uncomfortable, but you can always pretend they're someone else because, in a way, they were.

If I could twist enough to take a discreet selfie of my pitiful little flower (which looks more like a butterfly, searching for sky), I'd send a snapshot to you. Because I've been memoiring like crazy these days, and this piece of me will fit nicely into my confessional (though not apologetic) pages. You know me too well in person and haven't read my memoir yet, but I envision a day when you, plus my future great-grandchildren and great-greats, will read my sometimes clumsy words and see an eccentric old broad they wish they could have known better. I'll keep digging up more pieces of our family stories and myths for you to archive. With more time and distance, maybe I'll be letting in just enough sunshine.

Nonfiction

Silver Singles Dating Bio

PENELOPE PAGE

Name: Penelope Page
Age: 72
Single (never married)

I'm an old bohemian crone, a relic from the 1970s, one of the Coffee, Tea or Me girls. I'm independent, politically liberal, and a feminist. I prefer animals to people; I shun responsibility and hate calendars, telephones, and social media. I adore a good martini (dry, two olives), good food, and being served.

In 32 years, I've lived on four continents and in six states. I've traveled too far and seen too much. I'm highly opinionated and care nothing for norms. Some mornings I spike my coffee with Baileys Irish Cream, and I may take several naps during the day.

I've never lived anywhere for more than five years, and my relationships generally last six months, longer if you're rich. The poor need not apply; I can be penniless alone.

I drive a twenty-one-year-old car with 200,000 miles on it and buy my clothes at thrift shops. My fashion sense vacillates between bag lady and Hobo chic, all in plus sizes.

I have enough money in the bank to sleep well at night but not enough to survive a coma. These days my books are my friends, and my art, my lovers. I think God is a woman, organized religion over-rated, marriage a prison, and children a trap.

I won't be your nurse, cook, or mother. Leave your Viagra and four-hour erection at home. The helpless need not apply.

Be brave. Call me.

~

Background for Dating Bio

A few years ago, my nieces thought I should apply to the Silver Singles Dating service. They were so persistent that I wrote this bio as a joke, gave it to them, and said, "Sure, sign me up." After reading my dating bio, they never brought the subject up again.

Short Stories

Fear of Emptiness

INDRA CHOPRA

"Where do you start someone's story when every life has more than one thread and what we call birth is not the only beginning, nor is death exactly an end?" —Elif Shafak, *The Island of Missing Trees*

SATNAM KAUR SNUGGLES DEEPER into the evanescent warmth of her borrowed parka. It is minus 35 degree Celsius with flurries weaving their gossamer web around her. She trudges on towards the housing estate gate to receive her seven-year-old granddaughter. The one-kilometer walk seems endless as her aching chilled bones refuse to sync with the multiple divergent voices in her head.

Lately small things seem so precious . . . the smile of a neighbor, her granddaughter wiping her spectacles or sneaking in her favorite sweet. In the present uncertainty everything seems fragile, vulnerable, the feeling of loss omnipresent.

"I am late today." The school bus would be arriving any moment and I do not want to give the daughter-in-law another opportunity to berate me. "Not till I wriggle out of this distrustful arrangement."

Her granddaughter's smiling face, as she alights from the bus, brings a reciprocal smile on hers and taking the heavy satchel she joins the other grandmothers eager for the afternoon converse of problems, ailments, gossip or share snippets of village lives back in India. Today was different and Satnam knew that the others could sense something was amiss. They gave her the space. Keeping a watch on her granddaughter, Satnam walks on, replaying the early morning scene in the kitchen, with her daughter-in-law screaming obscenities at her. For a moment she had been dumbstruck by the venom, the animosity, feelings that must have been multiplying since the time Satnam had come to live with them.

At seventy-five, she could no longer single handedly manage household chores as she had, decades back, in India. She had tended to the fields, livestock, the household, her mother-in-law, an aging husband, and their only son. Her eyes misted remembering her marriage at age sixteen to a forty-year-old widower. Her family was penniless, refugees of the 1947 Partition of India. With no land or house or livelihood they married her off to the first eligible man. She does not blame them as during the horrific Partition days of killings and rapes, it was for the best.

Satnam looks up at the ominous gray winter clouds. They are just like her thoughts: mutinous. The screeching shrewish voice reverberates in the gentle breeze. "You have to choose between me and her." The overnight dirty dishes in the sink had triggered the verbal volley. Even though she had tried explaining, it had no effect.

The litany continued, cursing ungrateful parents, the burden on one person's salary when she, the daughter-in-law, had no time to look beyond her painted face and gaudy dress, chatting with mother and friends the whole day long. Her son was a spectator, refusing to meet her eyes. Blaming him would not help knowing that he was beholden to his wife for his "Kaneda" (Canada) citizenship.

Satnam looked at the other ladies realizing that her sole friend and confidante in this cold city was missing. Probably her arthritis must have flared up. The two friends eagerly awaited these few minutes to share their aches and pains and loneliness, to giggle that "they were partners in crime," crooning Punjabi ballads evoking memories of harvest season.

Thinking of the harvest festival, her wan face lights up. It was the day her son had come to fetch her and she remembers the euphoria and excitement in her village. The Canada papers had taken more than two years. Finally, it all went through and she eagerly packed her few clothes, her copy of the Sikh Holy Book *Guru Granth Sahib* and a few knick-knacks. Her son had insisted that she sell the farm, the heavy brass utensils, the silver anklets and gold jewelry. She resisted as they were *Nishani* or memories of her ancestors. There was no choice when told that her ticket and stay would be costing money. She had broken her promise to her husband to never sell the ancestral property to pay for the son's dream of migrating to Canada.

She had been weak. It started with city college, coaching classes for the Canadian application, paying the agents for the Visa and ticket. It had not stopped there, as once in the "dream land" he would often demand money to buy clothes and shoes, to feed himself. The jobs were erratic till he met his future wife, a Punjabi Canadian or to him his "Citizenship ticket."

Her granddaughter is safely at home. In her room, Satnam is back in the past. Months before her husband's death her one constant dream, three nights in a row, was of a green snake, comatose, looking at her. She did not tell her husband, fearing that he would laugh at her. After his death, she confided in her neighbor who told her that green snake dreams augur good luck. Maybe this explained her eagerness to fulfill her son's Canada dreams.

It was luck or simply fate that events played out to her son's script. She was the sole custodian of the land and house. It had not been easy warding off the claims of uncles and cousins, so it was easy to sell them. She consoled herself with the idea that her son had escaped to Canada and a life of plentitude.

The years zoomed past, a blur now, and here she is in this impassive, freezing land, desperate for some warmth from nature and acquaintances. It had not been easy adjusting. Her daughter-in-law was least helpful, making her arrival in Canada a favor. In return, Satnam managed the house, continuation of her life from back home, one drudgery after another. Nights were worse when she would stay awake for hours massaging her feet or weep herself to sleep, muffling the sound in her pillow.

The Kaneda lifestyle looks amazing from afar and one cannot blame the youngsters and parents in Punjab and other parts of India succumbing to false hopes. Every year the numbers keep on increasing, of youngsters lured by accounts and pictures sent by their friends little realizing that it was all chimeric. The stresses of lifestyle, language, cultural disparities, visa issues, loneliness leading to mental repercussions. She remembers her village neighbor receiving desperate letters from her son asking for money. A mistake the friend regretted later when she lost her son to drugs.

Mothers, like her, willingly contribute to the alienation of their children. They think they are helping in their future prosperity, but once they give in, they find themselves excluded from their children's plans.

The village women had made fun of Satnam that she would become a *mem-saheb*, a lady, wearing pants and shirts instead of her Indian clothes *shalwar kameez*. "Look at other matriarchs who had migrated to Kaneda. One can hardly recognize or understand their Canadian accented Punjabi or broken English."

She looks at herself in the full size mirror . . . the pants are there but not on a *mem-saheb*.

~

She shuts the world of loneliness and drudgery, transporting herself to the ochre mustard fields, the tinkling laughter of village children as they chase the calves and goats across the field. She flips around to another time and decade, accompanying her parents across the new borders into another field in another village surrounded by new friends and neighbors, recreating the old in new settings. This is a similar situation, crossing borders of soil and heart, adjusting with the borrowed mantle of her mother and aunts.

Satnam gets up to fetch herself a glass of water and hears her daughter-in-law's screechy soul-destroying voice, "I can no longer live with that witch."

~

The amber shades of dawn light up Satnam's steps over the threshold. She needs to get back to herself, to regain her *wajood*, or self-esteem, as her elders said. Her life had come full circle, from trivial to substance and now trivial again. She knows that grief has no boundaries and a person can find refuge anywhere as the world is ephemeral. . . . from the fields of what is now Pakistan, across the border in India and now Canada.

The *gurudwara*, Sikh temple, is her refuge from a lonely life and an opportunity to meet with other "discarded" souls like her. There was a talk about a senior's program where they were planning to provide refuge and care if someone desired. Satnam was eagerly awaiting it as she knew that her stay in her son's house was limited and she had no home in India.

The gurudwara's doors are open and she walks in with gratitude. . . ."*Toon Samrath Saran Ko Data Dukh Bhanjan Sukh Ra-e*" - "You are the Almighty Bestower of Protection, the Defeater of Distress, and King of Joyous Comfort."

Something Personal

Miriam Karmel

"It isn't personal," he tells her, not even glancing up while he sorts papers into piles: *keep, toss, maybe.* Glaring at the growing third pile, she sets the receiver back in its cradle, her ears still ringing, as if her daughter had slammed down her receiver, only Phoebe's teensy phone is flat, smooth as glass. Still, the insult of the sudden dismissal had the full-bore sound of a plastic-on-plastic head-on collision. It sounded personal.

Now *her* phone was made for slamming, though that's not her style. They've been through a lot together, she and her phone. She remembers when they called to say her sister was gone, and she forgot to hang up. Later, when Henry came home, he yelled, *Jesus, Ada! Don't you have anything better to do than sit on the phone all day?* Over the years, she's received wrong numbers, solicitations from the policemen's union, and once someone called to ask her opinion about something or other. You want her opinion? She prefers her old clunker to that itsy widget from which her daughter just terminated their conversation.

At some point, her daughter had said something about being stressed. Or perhaps she was getting dressed. No, Phoebe was stressed and said she might be coming down with something. She didn't think it was H1N1. More like a cold. Either way, she wasn't feeling tip top. And a friend was coming to visit. She simply didn't have time for her brother. But then a truck roared by,

68

its siren drowning out whatever came next. Could her daughter really have said, "Why can't he stay in a motel?"

Whatever was or was not said, the conversation turned. A truck passed by, a few words fell between the siren's blare, she couldn't hear herself think, and then, Bam! There you had it: the start of an unrelenting cascade of misunderstanding.

She suggested that Phoebe get a grip, find a way to handle her stress, which sounds like solid, motherly advice. If only she'd remembered that Phoebe is all grown up, has a life of her own. She even follows Martha Stewart, for whom everything is a big deal, from the thread count in sheets and pillowcases, to the spritzing of lavender water on a freshly made bed. *Step number one: Grow your own lavender.* Anyone contemplating all that in advance of a friend's visit might hang up.

She can't even remember the reason for Phoebe's call. Maybe it was a butt-dial. (How she loathes that expression.) Or maybe it was just a dutiful call to the old crone. She imagines Phoebe penciling her in: *Call Mom.* Now she wishes she hadn't said, "Really, Phoebs. It's no big deal to let a brother crash on the sofa for a night. No biggie." *No biggie?* Who wouldn't hang up?

When the phone rang she wondered whether it could be the call she'd been waiting for. Not that she had any particular caller in mind, only some free-floating idea of a voice that would tweak her mood, give her a lift, dare she say, change her life? Something serendipity. *Surprise me!*

She's given up on Publisher's Clearinghouse and even the MacArthur Foundation. This year's geniuses were just announced, and he, who continues tossing more papers onto that third pile, has pointed out that she must not have been home when the call was made, so those folks at MacArthur moved on down the list. LOL! But it might have been Trader Joe's saying they'd plucked her name from a jar of chits with the names of all the shoppers who toted their own bags to the store and she'd won fifty dollars for her effort. Trader Joe's was a distinct possibility.

Of course she wasn't expecting a call from her father, who, even if he could remember her number, would never call to apologize for slamming the phone down after saying, *I never want to hear from you again.* Dementia, she's been told, can trigger incivility, which reminds her of the guy who blamed *his* bad behavior on Twinkies. Shot someone dead, then pleaded insanity by junk food.

Nothing personal, the Twinkies made me do it. Nothing personal, he's demented. Nothing personal, I'm stressed and coming down with something that isn't H1N1, but is definitely something. Truth is, the insults feel personal.

And there, across the room, sits Henry, Mr. I'm-Going-to-Organize, Mr. De-clutter, Mr. Get-My-Life-in-Order, sifting through old papers while dispensing unsolicited advice. *It isn't personal.* And now he who just moved something from *toss* to *keep* offers, "Try letting it go."

She eyes the phone. The original number is still there in the center of the rotary dial. The print has faded, but squint and she can still make it out. Friends are charmed that it begins, not with an area code, but with the first two letters of the old exchange. *You're a dinosaur, Ada!* She remembers when Phoebe was barely tall enough to reach the receiver, the way she picked it up and said, *Juniper eight, four, four hundred.* She should call Phoebe and say, *Everything you did, even the way you answered the phone, filled me with joy. You were better than chocolate mousse, better than the first peonies of June, better than the wren that nested on the front porch every spring.* Yes, she could call, patch things up. Or maybe she'll stare at the phone, will it to ring, will some serendipitous something personal just for her.

Attraction

CARYN COYLE

HALLE SEES HIM AT the luggage turnstile. They must have been on the same flight. The man standing ten feet from her is tan, of course. They've just come from Florida.

Halle is right in front of the turnstile's opening, waiting for her suitcase to tumble out. She glances at him again, quickly and thinks that she recognizes him after, what? Thirty? Thirty-five years? He was twenty and she was three years older. Tall, with a full head of salt and pepper hair, he is leaner than she remembers him.

Does he recognize her? Halle doesn't think so. She has aged, too, though she believes she looks younger than she is. Halle is wearing a new t-shirt she bought on vacation – with the name of the town she visited on it – wondering if the man she recognizes has noticed her in it. It has a scooped neck and it is cut so that she hopes it accentuates her trim waist.

There is a dark haired woman next to him. She wears a linen jacket with navy piping. An expensive-looking, leather carry-on hangs over her shoulder. Halle notices that the dark haired woman stands just close enough to him to claim him. She is probably his wife. Halle glimpses a sparkle, a big stone, on the woman's left hand, ring finger. She lifts her eyes from the woman's hand and is annoyed that the woman is watching her.

Halle wonders if it really is the man she remembers. She thinks so. He never looked comfortable in his tall, full frame. He still doesn't.

Halle liked him, enjoyed his company and she can remember the night they met. They sat near each other in a neighborhood tavern. He told her that he approached her on a bet.

He didn't mention the bet as a "come on." He talked about it as though he was embarrassed. Shy. His honesty was charming.

"I don't know how to talk to women."

"Sure you do," she'd shaken her head. "You're doing it right now."

"Yeah, but they bet me I couldn't."

"Who?"

He stopped talking, his mouth a tight line.

Was it the way he said it that made him believable? Endearing? Halle can't remember.

He still looks uneasy. He is standing with his arms crossed, scowling; his back to the dark haired woman who has moved even closer to him.

Her fondest memory of him involved a blizzard that covered everything in more than a foot of snow. They'd been on a few chaste dates by then, nothing more than a quick kiss good night at her door. Somehow, with all that snow, he managed to get to her and dig her out. After clearing a path in her circular driveway, he made a fire in the ancient fireplace in her living room. Halle rented the wing of an old mansion. She lived in what had been the mansion's kitchen. A long wood paneled hallway had been built to connect it to the main house.

She remembers the snowy evening as festive, but not romantic. They sat on a rag wool rug in front of the large, brick hearth. It was actually large enough for someone to stand in it, and they probably did, two hundred years before. The hearth always made the room smell, faintly, of burnt firewood.

Halle's bedroom was a floor above the hearth, but they never climbed the stairs. They undressed while the fire snapped, hissed, and warmed them on the rag wool rug. She could sense his interest in her was more than hers for him. The imbalance wasn't uncomfortable. She would not have slept with him if it had been.

His skin was fair, like a child's. Blonde down covered his chest. With him, Halle felt that anything she did was admired. She was worthwhile. Significant. But his admiration was not enough. She wanted passion. Excitement.

Now, she has neither. Halle feels like her life has shrunk. She has too many empty minutes.

At the airport turnstile, the man Halle believes she knows is reaching for a suitcase. The woman is still right beside him.

"That's wrong," Halle hears her say. The woman's voice is shrill, high. It is not attractive and though she is definitely talking to the man Halle thinks she knows, he does not appear to hear her. He has placed the large suitcase, black – just like a million others – next to him and has pulled out an iPhone. He is staring at it, ignoring her.

"It's not yours, darling," she says, yanking on a tag attached to the handle. "Look."

He does not respond.

"Mike!" she says, loudly.

It *is* him. Halle suddenly remembers his name: Mike Buckley. She watches him shrug as the woman lifts the black suitcase and plops it back on the turnstile.

Halle smiles. Mike Buckley. She wonders what life would have been like if she'd felt differently about him. If her desire for him had matched his for her. Would her life have been better if she'd married him? Could she have been happy with the security and comfort his income would have provided?

Halle lives from paycheck to paycheck, sometimes not even that. She bought her ticket to Florida with the money she was saving to replace her twelve-year-old car. It has 176,000 miles on it. Though she stayed with her sister, for free, Halle still wound up spending more than she planned. She treated her sister and brother-in-law; dinner, drinks, she bought the t-shirt she is wearing and a sundress, a framed photograph of the Gulf of Mexico at sunset. Then she bought a gift card from the photograph shop as a thank you for her sister and brother-in-law.

On several nights, the three of them sipped Guinness in a pub on the main street of the town. They listened to a sixty-or-so-year-old guitar player who flirted with young women between songs. Sitting in a corner of the pub, under a bust of Jack Kennedy, he assumed an air of superiority. A cap hiding his thinning hair, he perched on his tall stool and ignored Halle, who felt invisible. Worthless.

Her suitcase pops up in front of her; light green. She pulls it off the turnstile and Halle is aware of Mike Buckley standing beside her. She catches his eye as she turns to set her suitcase down.

"Do we know each other?" Mike Buckley nods at her.

Halle blinks. She is on the cusp of explaining who she is when the dark haired woman encircles his left arm with both of her hands. Her wedding ring gleams in the airport's fluorescent light.

"Excuse us," she sneers.

Halle surprises herself and says, directly to Mike, "It's me, Halle!" She watches his eyes and only his eyes, ignoring the woman. Halle wants Mike Buckley to remember her. To regret the loss of their romance. From what she's seen, she believes Mike and the dark haired woman are not compatible. Maybe he is ready for a new life.

A life that includes Halle.

The dark haired woman's nostrils open and she inhales, silently. She continues to stand between Halle and Mike Buckley.

"Halle!" Mike smiles. He glances down at the woman's hands on his arm and then up at her face. The woman releases him. Mike steps toward Halle, "How are you? God, you look great!"

He engulfs her in a hug. He smells of peppermint.

"It's been a long time," Mike murmurs into her ear.

"MIKE!" the woman's words are loud. Severe.

He releases Halle, "I better go." Mike tilts his head slightly at the woman as if to say, *I'm in trouble now!*

Halle watches them walk away, their backs toward her. The woman leads. Her espadrilles slap the concrete floor with each step. Mike follows, picking up his pace to match hers and turns once to look back at Halle. He winks at her and grins before he turns away.

Walking as gracefully as she can manage, Halle lifts her head, pushing her shoulders back. She is grateful when a couple separates so that she can steer her luggage between them.

At the airport's sliding glass doors, a man who was watching his iPhone, looks up. He takes her in as she glides past him, out the doors that automatically open for her. Outside, the cold hits her, stinging her eyes. She is shivering in her t-shirt and her hands, without gloves, feel like ice.

A Sunday Intrusion

NANCY WERKING POLING

AN ALARM GOES OFF. I panic. Everyone on the cruise ship is racing to board a lifeboat. Some time during that scramble I realize it's not an alarm to abandon ship but the buzz of my front doorbell, that I've fallen asleep while watching a Raiders-Bears football game.

Foggy-eyed I head for the door, peer through the window, and regard six teenagers. Well-scrubbed kids, all of them white, three girls and three boys. I open the door, gaze up and down the street through the top of my bifocals. No cars in sight.

"Hello, ma'am," a tall, perky girl with a ponytail says. "We're from a church up in Philadelphia, and we're collecting cans of food for the poor." The boy beside her lifts a plastic bag. Either I'm at the beginning of their route or my neighbors aren't generous.

"Would you like to donate?"

Now, why are six teenagers from Philadelphia collecting food a hundred miles from home when wealthy suburbs surround their own city? From my TV set come cheers, like somebody's made a touchdown. I say what I hope will send these kids on their way.

"I donate to our local food bank."

A boy in a stocking cap steps forward. His tone is respectful. "We'd like to ask you a few questions, if you wouldn't mind."

"Shoot, but make it snappy."

"Do you go to church?"

Oh no. Clean-cut white kids going door-to-door instead of nesting in bedrooms with technological gizmos. No wonder I don't see a car; they probably came down here in a bus, wanting to convert us all to—to what?

"Yes," I reply curtly.

"Which one?"

"It's down that way." I point to the south.

Another girl, short and on the plump side, steps forward. "What two words would you use to describe your relationship with God?"

I've never been one to reduce thoughts to a few words, especially when it comes to issues of religion or patriotism. I repeat incredulously, "Two words?"

The six stand there staring at me expectantly. It's cold and I want to get rid of them. "Life-long—though it's one word." My curt tone is supposed to signal that the interview is over.

The boy in the stocking cap sticks his torso partway through the door. "What is your concept of God?" he asks.

I remember being their age, positive I had this God business figured out. I don't want to get into telling the truth, that the older you get the less sure you are of anything. That simple answers don't cut it anymore. But if I say anything about God as an ambiguous presence—*if* such a presence exists—who doesn't necessarily know everything and isn't powerful enough to have kept the Nazis from killing Jews or protect women in abusive marriages—if I mention such ideas, I'll be spending the rest of the afternoon with these kids.

"I'd rather not answer that."

A girl reaches in and grabs the sleeve of my sweatshirt. Our eyes meet, hers dark, piercing, insisting on more than perfunctory answers to questions on a clipboard. She wants honesty, I can tell. Something in what she's being taught doesn't resonate with her. She wants an adult who's not her pastor or youth leader or parent to speak honestly.

I grew up in the fifties, not all that great an era if you were female. Especially if you had doubts. If your father, instead of encouraging questions, offered pat answers. Question: Why would a loving God tell Abraham to sacrifice Isaac? Answer: It was to test Abraham's obedience. Obey your father; obey God the Father.

The girl clutching my sleeve reminds me of my friend Linda. The time we sat cross-legged in the middle of her double bed, hair in curlers, discussing the Meaning of Life. Linda stood and walked over to the window. She turned to face me, her voice quivering.

"Do you know what a lesbian is?" she asked.

"Yeah."

"I am one. I have a girlfriend. Do you think I'll go to hell?"

For me a chasm suddenly materialized between God the judge who sent people to hell and God who loved and protected everyone. It was the latter one I acknowledged as I sat on Linda's bed. "No, I don't think you'll go to hell." And I meant it.

But people at church turned against her, told her to her face that she should repent. She quit coming to church, and Daddy wouldn't let me spend time with her anymore.

All of these memories come to me while the girl still grips my sleeve and peers into my eyes.

"We'd like to keep you in our prayers," a boy says. "Do you have any concerns we can pray about?"

Pray for my retirement fund, I want to say, that it won't run out. Pray my old Jetta doesn't croak. Pray that the planet won't be destroyed by global warming.

Pray for Linda, that she found a partner worthy of her and that they live in a friendly place where her gifts are affirmed.

"No, not really." I step back inside the door to signal that I'm finished. The strangers thank me and turn to leave. The girl with the piercing dark eyes briefly lingers.

I sense her disappointment. She wanted me to speak with honesty. I've chosen to return to the football game.

Confession

LENORE HIRSCH

I HAD THE NIGHTMARE almost every night. I regretted what I'd done but I couldn't take it back. The only way I could imagine easing those memories was to confess. Not to the priest behind his dark curtain. And certainly not to the police. But what about Gramm?

When I was a kid and Mom and Dad went out, Gramm would come over to babysit me. She baked cookies—Mom never had time to bake cookies. She read me stories and gave me bubble baths. I had fun with Gramm.

The compulsory visits to Gramm's became annoying when I was a teenager. I loved her, but I hated having to go to her house when I would rather be with my friends. I treasured memories of our times together, but I had more important things to do.

Since leaving home, my visits to Gramm are rare. I still love her, but she's old . . . and I'm busy. Trying to make my own way. So I see her only once in a while. In recent years, it's been even harder to be around her. It's probably basic senility that comes from being ninety-something years old, but it's challenging. She forgets everything. She asks me the same questions and tells me the same stories several times in a half hour. Her apartment feels like a sauna; I can't stand being there for longer.

I got this idea that, well . . . if I could tell Gramm . . . maybe I'd feel better. I drove over there on a Saturday afternoon, a knot in my stomach. Could I do it? I took the elevator up and inhaled the usual mix of cooking smells in the hall. She welcomed me with a hug and we sat down at her kitchen table while the kettle boiled water for tea. She looked OK. Her hair was combed, her dress clean. There was no point in delaying.

"Gramm, there's something I want to tell you."

"Sure, Honey, you can tell me anything you want."

"I've never told this to anybody, Gramm. And it . . . you know, I dream about it every night. I just . . . need to find a way to make the nightmares go away."

She reached over and put her hand on mine. "What is it, Honey?"

"Well, it's about this guy. Do you remember? I dated this guy named Charlie."

She nodded. Maybe she met him once or heard about him from me or Mom.

"We were not a good match. We fought all the time. He . . . didn't understand me . . . and he wanted to be the boss of everything and . . . I didn't know how to get out of the relationship. So . . . there was this one time that we were fighting . . . and he slapped me. He slapped me hard and I . . . I couldn't believe it. I . . got away, but I didn't have the guts to break it off with him. I said to myself, though, 'If he ever does that again, I'm going to—I'll stand up to him—I'm not going to let him hurt me.'"

Gramm got up to get the whistling kettle. I wiped the sweat off my face and tried to slow my breath while she poured the tea and brought the cups to the table.

The earthy scent of chamomile drifted up from my cup. "Are you still with me?" I asked.

"Sure, dear. The awful boyfriend. I hope you broke up with him."

I studied the clock on the wall. The ten minutes that had passed seemed like an eternity. I continued. "Well, not quite. So there was this other time. It was summer and it was hot and we were out . . . we'd driven out to this park. We were fighting about something . . . I don't know. And he got really mad . . . and he tried to grab me . . . and I just—I remembered that slap. I remembered what I'd promised myself. And I pushed him. It wasn't like I pushed him that hard. We'd been drinking and he just . . . lost his balance . . . and he fell . . . and he hit his head on something. And there was blood coming out of his ear. And he was unconscious. I ran. I ran for—I don't know—for half an hour or forty minutes. I ran all the way home. And I snuck into the apartment all quiet, so as not to wake my roommate. And I went to my room and never told anybody."

Gramm was quiet. She was leaning forward, eyes closed, forehead strained, like she was in deep thought.

"I don't know what else to say, Gramm. I didn't call for help . . . I found out later . . . that he died. It was an accident, but . . . you know . . . maybe . . . maybe I could have saved him. And I don't know if there was an investigation. I know people, some people knew that we were seeing each other, but he was just found there in the park with his car, and nobody asked me anything. I'm sorry, Gramm." I took a sip of tea, but my throat was so tight, I choked.

She opened her eyes. I examined her expression, trying to know whether she had even heard it all.

"Gramm?"

She looked at me. I noticed dark circles under her eyes. "I don't know, dear. Seems like a terrible thing to have happened. Is there somebody you can tell now?"

"I'm telling *you*, Gramm. I need to be able to sleep. You've got to promise me you won't repeat this to anyone."

She nodded and smiled. We drank our tea. She forced me to take a tin of stale cookies with me. As I grabbed my jacket to leave, she patted my shoulder. "Darling, was there something you wanted to tell me?"

I drove home with the window down, clearing my head. I went to bed. And I slept. Those nightmares I had, they were always about that push, about the smell of liquor on his breath and the warm night and the buzzing in the trees and that push. Only, in my dreams, he'd fall back and the earth wouldn't be there and he'd just be falling through the sky and falling and falling and I'd be crying and calling him. So I had that dream again after I told Gramm, but this time it was different. This time he floated to the ground. And he stood up. And he walked away.

Poetry

Organs

STELLA BRICE

I have come back at last to my old garden. It has grown
up in my absence—yellow plums, high grasses, a snarl of
violets & loosestrife, dogwood & redroot & a stand of
hot pink, thorn-chased roses.

My neighbor, Mrs. Nymph, has tended the garden in the wake
of the abandonment. (The ancient gates wrenched open for
anyone to master.) She wears her gray-blonde hair in a
chignon. Her grandmother's rotting mink hangs on her frame.
The monogram of that debutante missy is embroidered in golden
thread on a secret pocket in the intimacy of the sweat-tanged
drape of the shredded scarlet satin lining.

Mrs. N. lends her strict hand to this wanton articulation.
But she only barely subjugates. . . .

If the juice of these diverse plants, if all the juice—
malign & beneficent—is dropped into my eyes, it does clear
my sight. The umbels of the flowers burble large & many-rayed
& the fruit spreads very broad wings. A quarry of names &
faces push, nest & crawl in & out with undulations. The dirt
is shot half-through with random shoots. It is riddled with
organs of light.

SOAR Studio

Suzanne Freeman

A rat-turd hermitage
home to Cass and her cob-webbed wares,
Shadow of a Rainbow sagged backward
from New Mexico 90. Her inventory
of unsold stumps stretched clear to the road,
while inside the sooty adobe
a chain-smoking sentry waited for customers
with a worn-out hound named Bama. Together
they guarded a tray of painted gourds,
the overpriced baggies of scavenged piñones,
some desiccated cobs of corn
re-kerneled with glue and tiny crystals. Few tourists
were lured by the hand-lettered sign
that leaned against the mailbox
--Crystals*Dog Grooming*Sculpture--
and she frightened with her bug-eyed tales
of banditry, of dope flooding in from Mexico:
You came at a bad time.

Regal in short-shorts
on muscular gams that were tan as a saddle,
she'd stride through the village barefooted,
bare-headed in high desert sun,
her straight-up hair bone white

like the teeth she sometimes wore.
Pistol on her hip, chainsaw in her hand,
her mission nobody's business. (Scouting
for stumps? Scaring off *Yankees* and *snowbirds*?)
Some unlucky twilight
you might see her by the stream at the crossing
where she once spooked a horse, and then
you were in for more cigarettes and a sermon:
Put away that camera. Just listen to the trees.

Did the cottonwoods warn her that shadows
are dangerous when the rainbow caves in?
That she'd go out on a stretcher, felled
by a stroke and mute as a stump?
Do the junipers reminisce
about the cackle of "her kind," her cigarette
tracing a rainbow's arc in the darkness?

How Scotch Broom Came to Dallas

SUZANNE RHODENBAUGH

Margaret Carlisle: big loudtalking Texas woman
of oversized gesture, exaggerated drawn-out
Southernized story, including many many
unnecessary piled-on heaped-up
curlicued and yet emboldened
details. She was hail fellow well met
in female version: a big-haired, full-bodied,
way way elaborated, hyperdrawling got-up
Christmas tree of a woman.
And she wanted Scotch broom.

It might have been butcher's broom or moonlight broom.
Margaret called it Scotch broom.
She'd seen it on a hillside in Virginia
near the military school her son attended
and she was hell-bent on getting Scotch broom.
So she called Bonnie Drummond in Richmond
and made plain her heartfelt desire: a kind of
piney-bambooish-looking plant that bloomed
with yellow flowers – her description was
none too good. Bonnie looked it up and called around:

nobody had it, and nobody knew.
Then for Scotch broom Bonnie tried Monticello.
Well they had it, and they would provide.
Thus a horticulturalist for the floral legacy of Thomas Jefferson,
our genius President, a botanist, landscaper, farmer
and so much more, dug up two big Scotch broom clumps
and left them outside the greenhouse, and Bruce and Bonnie
hefted them into plastic bags two days later
and trucked them back to Richmond and kept them alive.
And then on two flights west – Richmond to Atlanta

to Dallas – Bruce carried Scotch broom in his arms,
and brought the clumps to Stewart, Margaret's
big, affable man, who with his wife's gardening buddies
planted Scotch broom in plain view, so that
Margaret Carlisle, before she died, would have before her
the modest little yellow flowers she loved and wanted in Texas.

Arlee

Suzanne Rhodenbaugh

We had tart cherries in chocolate, bitter pickled greens.
Sour apple ice cream, whopping onion rings.

And lamb very slowly roasted
at a cottage by a shaggy pond
somewhere in eastern Pennsylvania,
in the time after Arlee's famous husband
dumped her for a younger woman.

A divorce veteran myself, I was along
to help out Arlee and give her advice.

Now Arlee was freckled, wrinkled, unkempt,
and more or less beautiful.
She had a tendency to xerox.
An East Texas redneck
with an M.D. degree, she had four
smart-mouthed daughters, an addiction
to causes, the messiest house I've ever seen
and a mop of fading red hair.

I thought Arlee should clean her house,
trim her fingernails and toenails,
straighten out those snotty kids

with a swat they were long overdue for,
sit her husband down and say *Fine.*
You go on and do what you're gonna do
but here's my price – in bucks –
and by the way, take the kids.

Arlee didn't do that
but Arlee sure didn't fold.

She spent that weekend on a crying jag,
worked a year as a clerk,
took a Greyhound bus to Arizona
and a pediatrics refresher course,
and commenced to care for Indian children:

Arlee in the desert with her big laugh,
her twang, and her kindness.

The Lady of the Garden

ELAINE NAMANWORTH

She sits
In her beauty
A thing apart
From all else
That is beautiful
Her smile
A thin crescent
A moon to wish upon
Her shoulders
Smooth and pale
Where her lovers
Heads have been
She does not speak of them
But when she speaks
The bones
Inside her face
Seem to take the shape
Of what she says
She tells of the search
For her double
Tossing her hair
As she laughs
It floats
Like sunslip
Into her afternoon

Dances
She sometimes dances
In gray velvet
Or naked
Where the garden ends
Never the same dance twice
Never the same motion
Of her hands
As they pull rhythms
From the air
Into her soft lengths

She knows magic
Lights around her senses
Flash
When she looks
She feels
She does not only see
When she throws off
Her white body
She is everywhere

She knows things
She dances
She laughs
But her dreams are sad

The Second Beauty

Elaine Namanworth

A splinter of sun
Split the orchard down the middle
Rested on her face
Chiseled ivory, oval shaped
Revealed her, shiny as a daystar
In multiples of blue
The sky, the veined hands, the eyes
With lines at the corner points
The first one came too soon
Right after she made the child disappear
The next one when the child vanished by itself
Another showed following the fire
Big hot teeth ate her paintings
While she slept like a cat
On the chest of her soldier
Dreaming of water
Five creases formed after the war
Parallel lines appeared
Like an obscene musical staff
Carved above her cheekbone

The second beauty is a powerful thing
Jagged and brambled and owning no secrets
Imperfect, brave, accessible
With a certain noble loveliness

Sometimes, remembering her first face
She let herself laugh
Making young girl sounds
Little bells
Only certain birds could hear

She carried her history on her face
In open glint and glisten
The light she absorbed and the light she gave off
Intertwined
Something jingled where she stood
Strange birds gathered where the fallen apples were

Spinster

Claudette Mork Sigg

Years ago we found a coffee can of marbles
stashed in ivy growing in our backyard.
The ivy was unrelenting, born from winter rains
and sunshine filtering through oaks
into a garden gone wild.

We were young ourselves then,
wilder than we are now,
and we pulled out of these round stones of agate
tales glowing with swirls of color
rolling, falling, and caught between our fingers
like thread spinning from a shuttle into tapestry.

These days, the most beautiful nestle in a handblown bowl
on the coffee table in the sunlit living room.

Sometimes I pick up one, a swirling blue one
with oceans surging on its surface.
"Tell me a story," my grandchild asks, as I stare into it.

"Once upon a time, there was a girl,
a very little girl, and one day she found herself
beside the sea."

"Was there a boat on the beach?"

"Yes," I said. "And on that day that little girl began the journey of her life on an ocean filled with wondrous things, like seals . . ."

The marble with the blue swirling sea in it spun out the tale, and my little girl and I went sailing into that sea.

Matriarch in the Garden of Bees

CLAUDETTE MORK SIGG

There was a time when men saw king bees
buzzing in hives, flitting out into sunshine,
driven from blossom to blossom,
their backs loaded with pollen,
like the Diego Rivera painting
of a man bowed to the ground
under a heavy load of flowers on his back,
the woman's job a minor one of steadying his burden.

There are men who go into false labor
when the birth pains begin
and she takes a struggling breath to prepare
for the long job of pushing life out of her body.

Back in the very beginnings
before men descended from trees to begin running in the grasslands,
what did they, these glorious monkeys, know of anything important
when the magic of birth seemed all her own?

Spear points fastened to shafts,
dead mastodons, and meat on the slab—
that was a man's job.

As it turned out, all the worker bees were females
under the rule of a golden matriarch,
drones tolerated for the mating flight
and then, like Icarus, for their presumption,
allowed to fall, emasculated, to earth.

Frida Kahlo never gave over her hand to his grasp
in the wedding portrait she painted of herself and Diego—
it's her brush, not his, that created this work,
a vision born in her woman's brain,
a queen bee secure in the honey-hive of her imagination.

Garden Walk with the Chairmaker's Wife

CINDY RINNE

Zebra shawl covers her clay mind
Cat gently brushes shin
Carmen draws near to text on the chair he made
Glides her hand along the arm where his rested
Thinks about the meaning of *chair*

Down the path, she ties red ribbons on sage plants
Hosts the spiral snake
at the cyanotype edge of stacked stones
Waterfall splashes a pendulum of snowmelt
Earthworm respects the water source

Silken cherry blossoms fall like lace
Kuan Yin undergirds the crows' wisdom song—
Listen to the message inside your skin
Your body is sound
Interconnect with all life

Carmen hears the goddess ring the gong
Vibrations lull baby shells in abalone cocoon
Bleached claws reach for the children
Pink crystal web protects in woven shadows
Wind reshapes holes across brittlebush

Beneath sun's rays of sequins, a leaf evolves
on a willow where the Bennu Bird resides
Carmen breathes through the loneliness
Five quick outbreaths
One long, until lungs are empty

She gathers lemon balm, lavender, and mint
Kneels at the pearl altar
Yellow candle lit
Places herbs and an egg at the roots
Carmen desires to touch the sawdust of his hands

Home: Winter Crossroads

CINDY RINNE

Firewood smoke snakes across the canyon.
Birds chatter. A golden weave of leaves
vibrate in twilight's shiver. Snowmelt gushes.
A gurgling stream like waters in my belly.

The torn edges of fear, loss, despair
devour the broken bowl of my body.

Dhumavati, crone of letting go, instructs:
Get rid of 27 objects each for nine days.
I sort through jewelry, books, and clothes.
Say, *thank you.* Liberate the memories.

Release who I was
to become who I am.

Hecate encourages be a silent witness.
Strong shelter for my words. A home aglow.
In my room, I sweep a path under a bridge
for glass fish in a miniature Japanese sand garden.

Add stone, shell, and coral.
A map of a sacred solstice site.

What Gathers In

ANITA PINATTI

The crone knows.
She knows the push and pull
of pedals on the loom.
She can be a magpie
searching for scraps of silk
to weave into flowers.
She might be a goddess,
Diana pointing the way.
She gathers bark from birches
the way I gather poems.
We drink from the same stream
where my heart slips in,
annealed.
She cleans with an owl's feather.
They sing in the dark.

Deconstructed Soup

ANITA PINATTI

It being just morning, flowers droop a subtle warning.
The air goes flat. Night fragrances slowly dissipate.
Dank and bitter roots swim through jars along my
windowsill.
Spring onions poke through holes in my pocket.
Polar ice is melting. Bears are sinking.
Retinal vein occlusion looks like scribble on a page.

I Still Get Hunger

SUSAN CAVANAUGH

The outliver, I am filled with a guilt
I work to turn. I still get

peaches from Sunny Slope Farms
in August, cider in October.

I still have that map of Atlantic City,
I still get beach, boardwalk, blue sky,

casinos, pizza, cheesesteak subs.
I still get to try to come close

to the pesto, tabouleh, tide pool
soup, prized dishes of family,

friends, neighbors from a dozen
old addresses decades in the past.

I still get to Tony's Produce,
gallons of orange juice,

still get to plunge my hands
into fresh lettuce, unsure

how without you I will
make fine salads. And I do.

Kitchen Crumbs

Ronna Magy

If you find me in childhood's kitchen again,
    rolling pin, mixing spoon, porcelain bowl.
If you find me curled inside grandmother's apron,
    her gnarled fingers kneading soft cookie dough.
If you find me twirling a flour dusted glass,
    dough rounds placed on a pot metal sheet.
And father comes home yelling, slamming the door,
    money, the clients, adding machine days.

If you find this child
    crouched under kitchen table's legs.
If you see a woman's wrinkled hands
    quivering over a sink.
If a man's enraged voice
    shudders the walls.
Wall clock's dial isn't moving at all.

Strew a cookie crumb trail outside the back door.
    Bang wooden bowls, knock down kitchen walls.
Call neighbors and friends so everyone hears
    women's shaking and freezing, silent waiting out time.

Burn kitchen's pot dry.
    Leave nothing behind.

Tree

JEANNE BRYNER

Gales, what lies ahead for her, for us
we call an arborist, a doctor for trees
who himself has a *family emergency*.
I am a messenger, not a prophet, this story's
not the tale of Shishmaref, Alaska's melting
island, its ten houses swallowed by the sea
or how a committee of suits
pitch forked the flow of Chicago's river
sent sewage to the Mississippi. I am one
and hum to our tree when I gather my zinnias.
We are on a list, our number's written down.
To my eyes, the canopy is full, green, lush
her south limb bears some trouble, dark cracks
fissures widen, a fret, a worry. Scarred arms
stretch above the road so there's urgency.
They'll need to use the lift bucket, auger
a hole, check for softness of rot. Days
I walk the yard, I pause, stroke her blind face.
I know, I know it's not your fault.
If she can be saved, we want it done.
We'll not ask for a Dorcas miracle, just mercy
for our friend. Without our tree, this home ends
broiled in hell's sun. No wreath shall sign
her spot, no cross name her goodness

these eighty summers, winters all
years of bounty, years of none
Lady of Autumn, to my knees, I fall.

Midden

JEANNE BRYNER

To not gesticulate or fuss
about the weight
of wet sofa cushions
moonlight's apneic snoring.

To not question banishment
refrigerator hinges
begging doors
a holey sock, catatonic
from losing her mate.

To not grumble
about overcrowding
your smelly neighbors
piled on mattresses
of moldy bread.

To find meaningful content
decaying on hillsides
couplets of soup cans
running over
one verse into another.

To consider being dumped
as traveling to a faraway place
a blue satellite lands
on the bright planet
of empty ketchup bottles.

To not curse the squish
of half-rotted peaches
to embrace the harmony
of leftover chicken bones.

To let the sun's kiss
bring comfort to legions
of one-eyed teddy bears
legless kitchen chairs.

To approach the end
smiling in your banana hat
not minding being simpler
lower, unimportant.

The Crone

ANA MARÍA CARBONELL

so wise
the shape of a body
no longer matters
wrinkles on a face
marks of honor

but the Iron Maiden lingers
each day, hour, second
we know exactly what she looks like
we feel the cage from hundreds of years ago

a great great aunt of mine died young
because her corset was too tight

German girls rotted in iron cells
today we soak in serums and dyes
lie lathered in lotions
some of us cut off our thighs
slice open our breasts
even pull up necks and eyes

Come, old Crone
I've heard of you—
they say we all become you.
When?

The Sentence

ANA MARÍA CARBONELL

In Spanish, we say *estoy enferma*. It means I'm sick.
I may be sick of this, but I am not *enferma*

In fact I am more alive than ever

In English we say we're on a punctuation mark.
Yet you can't be on something that ends a thought. Period.
And it prompts thought. A lot.

I am 54 and definitely still on it. But I can't say I'm "on it."
I can't say "Oh yeah, I got this"—Can you?

By now you either know what I mean or you don't
which is fine as long as if you don't
you don't say you do and you never *ever*
tell me I'm on it

On the upside they say it keeps my skin nice
which makes me wonder *How would I look without it?*
as I bathe, baste under creams, ointments, serums

It's obvious by now this isn't the end of a sentence.
It *is* the sentence—a very long one that wouldn't be so bad
if I could live it out in my own Red Tent

filled with bonbons, red wine, salty Trader Joe's chips
thicker, saltier, crispier than those Fritos lookalikes

on the edge of a beach in a parallel universe
where a shaman, *una bruja*, would tell me
chocolate, alcohol, Trader Joe's chips (not Fritos)
are just what you need at a time like this

She'd also tell me, crying when you hear Purple Rain
on the way to work is okay because your heart
does in that one second hold and bathe everyone—
your students, boys, and all the children you know and don't

Maybe this sentence, this very long sentence
allows me to travel far and wide
so I feel bubbling volcanic substances,
craggy, crumbling planets
in far-flung reaches of our universe

For fleeting moments I know
what it's like to be those planets
I know what needs to be done
while I barely hold on to my own body

If you are near me, I tell you what we should do
what you should do and make sure you don't tell me
what I should do because I know—because I'm on it

I am trying to hold dry earth in my hands
without it falling through my fingers
lava runs through my hot arms and legs

I am holding the universe together
I am trying to keep you with me
I am trying to keep everyone with me—

La Vieja

Mary Volmer

I hunger for the old woman I knew before I knew my name. You know who I mean. You've seen her in every park from here to Austin, wearing house shoes, feeding pigeons in the early morning and again when evening fades and the dark swallows her whole and turns pigeons into men.

Twisted trunk of a woman. Bramble hands. Every day, she kneads the bread that will become manna. Give her a sniff if you wonder where the yeast comes from. Oh, she scares old men, but children know it's she who stays behind with Ruth to gather herbs and grain in the wake of the reapers. They know the sound of her grinding stone late at night means bread in their bellies in the morning.

Last night, I saw her in the war-torn background of a news report, visible, but just, behind the correspondent's bright blue coat. There she was, making a stone oven out of rubble and talking (maybe praying) to herself, or to the pigeons all around, or to the ghosts of children who find her by the smell of bread. It was she who attended the mother's labor in the stable; who led her lost boy into the temple; who peeled the shroud from his body before she moved the stone. She lives. In Kyiv and Los Gatos, in Botswana and Paris, in Mogadishu and Orinda; at the foot of the mountain, she lives, and in the alleyway behind the pizzeria; she lives in the park, in the slums, in a hut near the dry riverbed in the desert valley. Look, she says, make bread from wheat, make bread from ashes. We were all born knowing how to starve slow enough to stay alive.

Bread in the oven. I hunger. She delivers me into my mother's hands, gathers grain and grinds it; wheat dust, bone dust, she is the leaven. I knew her before we knew my name.

Parable of the Oak

Mary Volmer

The black oak in my dreams, flourishing old ancestor,
with roots deep and wide as the hill on which she grows
and limbs outstretched in every weather.

Last night, after a difficult day in a series of difficult days,
I found her dying. Leaves, brittle and falling out of season,
carpeted the grass. Her trunk, dry and blighted.

For a long time—hours, years—a horrid, hollow
despair overwhelmed me, until, I don't know why,
I stood up and stepped away to look from a distance

at the oak who once renewed me. There, in her shadow,
I made a decision. I would not imagine death.
Even with death everywhere around me, I would

extend imagination to life and give life back to that
which nourished me. At first, sitting in the cradle
of her roots, I felt no change. Leaves fell. Branches fell.

Nothing changed. Until rattling wind softened
against the skin of one green bud. Then two. My fingers
greened. My feet grew roots; with roots I traveled

down, down into loam until my back, a scarred trunk,
bridged leaf and root. And when the fallow time had passed,
Oak and I, together with you and I, bore fruit again.

Stone Age

Jennifer L. Abod

On my walk,
I pick up one stone
different from the rest,
cup it comfortably in my hand.
Bluish gray, like a Civil War uniform,
oblong, like a tear drop,
the top, round and smooth.

In feathery white lines,
pointy pumpkin eyes appear.
Tiny pockmarks, a nose.
In the thick slash below,
a grin sneers, a skeleton's skull!

I study the hand
that holds the stone.

Ski-lines crease each finger,
deepen into ruts in the pink of my palm.
Mountain ridges ripple the stem of my thumb.
A bracelet of grooves circles my wrist.

I have been wondering
how to let go
the useless stones I carry.

I slip this death stone
into my pocket
to remind me how to let go
the useless stones
I carry.

Lesbian Crone

JENNIFER L. ABOD
inspired by Lucille Clifton's poem, *song at midnight*

Sisters,
do not send me out
among strangers*

Hair cropped purple
unkempt with distinction

I carry much strength
in the ravines of my thighs

Eyes
heavy lidded
crescent moons
still ignite rebellion

Sisters,
if you do not see me
beautiful
who will?

words inspired by Sonia Sanchez

For Carlos

TERRY A. ALLBRIGHT

We are invisible
Carlos told me he will disappear on his birthday
Because when you are 30, you are no longer seen
He said he can wear anything, anywhere
He can rob a bank and be indescribable
A ratty swimsuit at Deep Eddy Pool, now OK
Flat shoes, no one cares anymore
And the hair, who sees the hair?
I am the glasses frames not the face
I am the slow driver in the right lane
The turn signal flashing too soon
The birthday card in the mail
The gift card for Christmas
The grocery cart parked at the side of the aisle
The slow walker on the sidewalk
My friend is not entirely accurate, however
A young man does look through me in the store
But the old guy with blue eyes winks and smiles

Cake

Terry A. Allbright

Cita stands tall with the wind blowing her bright, white hair that turned when she was not yet 30.

She smiles and opens her arms to greet us, not saying she has been standing there for an hour.

All is well as we settle in, then the seams begin to tear and we cannot look away.

With coffee and cake, she asks, "Now tell me again what you named that new boy.

Jordan, Oh yes, now I remember. Jordan. Did you bring him?"

Our breath rasps against sandpaper in our chests as we try to appear unstartled. We did not know.

The new boy rests on our bed in the room where Mike slept until he left for Austin.

Cake eaten, she asks, "What is the name of that new boy? Jordan. Oh, yes, Jordan."

Again and again, the same question, again and again but the same answers do not stick.

She knows she cannot remember and cannot stop asking. She begins to cry and apologize.

Mike has to leave the room because she is his mother and he cannot bear the pain.

I stay and listen and answer and answer because I can. Jordan wakes, comes looking for cake.

Her eyes are saucers. She asks, "Who is the boy there, in the doorway? Do I know him?"

I hold out my hand and he walks toward us. He eats cake. "This is our Jordan, the new boy."

"What about the other boy you have? Do you still have him?"

"Yes, that is Blake. He is with Tommy at the station and will come here soon."

"Oh, OK. I am sorry. Now, what is the name of your other boy? And do I know Tommy?"

"Oh yes, Cita. That is our Blake and your Tommy, my oldest son and your oldest son."

"I have cake. Do you want cake? And coffee? Boys like cake."

In the Curve

PHYLLIS CARITO

In the curve of seventy
that's not too steep
but the arc is tight
and downhill into
the self again,
the efforts of progress
through the years
gliding toward who
and how you are
meet the cliché –
we become more of our-
selves as we age –
more tolerance
offset with less
patience,
still desire to engage
adventure and travel
offset with physical losses
in the long descent –
hearing and sight falter
knees and hips drag
passion is tempered –
in the curve hold on
to touch – that gentle embrace
of life itself.

Arise the Woman

PHYLLIS CARITO

I am part woman, part tree, part lion.
I know what I didn't before about
how we celebrate a woman,
pollute a tree, lose the jungle.

I hear the suffragettes and
women libbers echoes,
but where is my ability
to confront the opposite sex?

I know the pollutants are humans,
yet no lion leader roars in me.
I remain a follower
caged in my own limitations.

I burrow myself in a grove of trees
and mean to protect the land;
I breathe the air, sway with the wind
but can I share the bounty?

Where will I draw my power?
There is always a reminder
of weakness, and a fear,
unfounded and real as it might be.

I'm persuaded that the terrible ending
at each step is really a next beginning,
I know what I didn't know before
my pendulum always leaves me swinging;

I move away from hurt
to find a steady footing,
I embrace the tree and the lion
to save the woman again and again.

What Remains

Connie Levesque

I've got nothing to say about old women,
having lost the ones I used to know.
They left some quilts, a jewelry box,
a small glass dish for nuts and such.
And a cat. I can't forget the cat—
he won't let me.

I could tell you what they liked to read,
or how they took their tea,
or the way their bodies changed,
or how they went—
some sudden, some slow,
but what's gone is gone.

And what remains is an ache
as cold as the ocean,
a wave, all foam and fury,
that heaves against the shore.

When I fear I might drown
for want of their hands,
I grab that damned old cat,
and moored beneath the weight of him,
I marvel at how warm his belly feels
against my thighs.

Wild Sisters

CONNIE LEVESQUE

Were I elephant and aged,
I'd lead sisters, daughters, young
to water in times of drought,
to graze in times of plenty,
and when I died, I'd be mourned,
my bones caressed, remembered.

Were I honey bee and aged,
I'd dance my sisters to vibrant blooms,
to heather and clover, cat-mint and aster,
and pollen-laden, return to the hive,
until my wings, grown ragged,
could no longer carry me home

But I am human and aging,
I text my sisters, I tend my garden,
I fear that when I'm truly old,
body frayed like the wings of a bee,
we'll have lost the elephants,
and honey bees.

And when our wild sisters are gone
who, then, will dance among our bones?

Larkspur Trail

CAROL BARRETT

Pine boughs nod their whisking yes
to this noble exercise of heart
and song, this wind-swept walk along

a foaming creek that pulls north
like a drunken river, the walkers' arms
latched to torsos, ambling in rhythm,

hands hooked in loose seam, heads
cocked to the rush of water over wet
slate. A child in plaid skirt skips ahead

like a small stone tossed from the wrist.
A spaniel heads their way, bounding
beyond his master, pulling, intent

on covering the sun-smoked turf
before the sky can shift gears, settle
the doves in rafters, the quail in coveys

among the sage. The dog is happy
as the smell of barbecues
drifts through cedar slats. He makes

the walkers' faces light. When they began,
they did not know any of this:
girl, dog, bird, pine, stream. Only

that the body needs its ground,
its holy place in the fine dust of things.
Nuthatch nesting, they won't tell where.

Snowfall

CAROL BARRETT

A few days before I die
I'll shovel a thin ribbon
along the muffled walk
where old flowers
merge their snowy heads
in the thickening bed.
I'll stroke the library banister
long way down to the basement floor,
the record player spinning
its scratchy hymn. The "girls"
will be taking off their scarves,
unrolling thick beach towels
on the beige carpet, each
in her own space. I'll go
to the head of the class, greet
each pink face like a new poem,
begin with a shoulder roll, a brisk
whirl of the hands. Midway
we'll stop to rest. Someone
will put water on in the kitchenette.
I'll remember my grandmother,
rising each morning from the yellow
chenille to sit-ups on the hardwood
floor, then teach the younger women

things which pulse through us
when the shape of hips no longer
matters. We will coach each other
past funerals and broken wrists,
our bodies warming the chattering air.
Someone's granddaughter
will be visiting, her braids long
as the scarves. We will take turns
saying how quick she catches on,
her waist bending to a tender
compass. After the last
curled spine extends to the top
of the hour, we will sip tea
and stories, then pass through
the upper chambers where new books
gloss the round tables, my hands
pressed to the glass door
like a prayer, mittens disclaiming
imprint, the squeak sounding behind me
as the indelible snow takes over.

Passing Through

JOAN ANNSFIRE

I tap through this cyberworld,
where trails of keystrokes represent immortality.
This is who I am, who I have been:
much older now and writing
my obituary online.

I have no family left.
Parents long dead, one childless,
aging lesbian warrior;
pressing down cyber-grass
much like moving
through fields of tradition,

I leave indentations
like crop circles
marking distance traveled.

I cruise the information highway
looking for my legacy.
This road of imagination
where dreams are memorialized
alongside offhand comments,
spoken simply as soundbites,
throwaway lines.

Posts note only minutes spent,
ideas considered; vistas seen.
Links connect me to a human network,
a community displaying
accomplishment and artifice side by side;
brutal honesty woven with lies
and infused with great mystery.

Digital footprints declare
although I moved through this world unnoticed,
for just one brief click of time,
I passed this way.
I was here.

Musical Memory

JOAN ANNSFIRE

Music transports me.
to that peak of memory just above necessity,
ushering me back to a time
when family was a given
and all questions were new.

Childhood, for me, was not
a gentle place of care
but a steep wall I learned to scale
with expert precision.

My mother, self-taught on piano,
would play chords of show tunes
as my sister, father and I sang along,
If notes were fudged or missed altogether,
we just sang louder.

Her music proved a crescendo of power and magic,
spilling out beyond sorrow,
a long-guarded promise;
a dance moving me to the far edge
of possibility.

With this soundtrack
My life felt more like a movie.
A fierce cacophony of splendor,
destined for a cataclysmic ending.

Those were days of
precarious hope and artful balance.
My struggle, a mountain I would attempt to summit,
while avoiding fissures of malformed parenting
threatening each step.

Music transports me.
Especially when I'm most in the grip
of this merciless, difficult world.

Harmonious sound reverberates
deep as the vortex of time.
For one fleeting moment, evoking the past
Then trading it for a song.

Near Her Cauldron Where a She-Fox Leaps

KATHARYN HOWD MACHAN

for Barbara Walker

Wise Woman drapes herself in crimson—
the robe her mother wore until death—
and lifts a goblet of ruby glass
to praise the moon with Isis horns

high in clear black sky. Weather
is coming—a storm, hard winds, snow
that will cover and blind. But here
with her fire and her small red beast

she'll use her prayers to guide the lost
travelers in these cold wild woods
to find the homes that will keep them alive
at least this one dark night.

Dorothea's Hands

KATHARYN HOWD MACHAN

She clapped in the room of lavender.
Her single window let in light
that played across her simple afghan
where her fingers pushed and pulled soft threads
most hours of the day. *Dementia*:
how a ghost named Max
borrowed her clothes and made them bigger
and rearranged her decades of jewelry
and sometimes whispered her name.
Today I've come in silver sequins
and a long pale veil of silk.
I've danced for her as she used to dance
with me in our shared laughter.
And slowly, surely, her eyes watched
and a first smile graced her mouth.
She clapped in her room of lavender.
And I bowed before her love.

Mad for the Moon

GAY GUARD-CHAMBERLIN

I'm an unapologetic lunatic
for all things numinous
lovely and luminous

I'm fanatic for the fantastic
the phosphorescence
of bioluminescence

the opalescent essence
of moonlight in refraction
the knowing reflection

inside an abalone shell
its lustrous glossy gleams
like the iridescent dreams

of miniature moons
milky-pearl planets and crystal spheres
singing bowls for the waning years.

Cornucopia

GAY GUARD-CHAMBERLIN

On the anniversary of her death, again I dream
of my mother, her four adult children seated
in our old positions: north, south, east, and west,
around the big oak table.

To our astonishment, this is where we find her,
an odalisque-as-centerpiece—
reclining, regal, proudly on display,
her whole body encased in silver net.

Seeds and nuts spill out, cascading
from her hands, feet, mouth, and breasts.
The bounty overfills the plates and napkins,
falls like ripened fruit into our laughing laps.

"Eat," she says, without words, yet we hear.
Her shining eyes broadcast bliss
in her new role as vessel
for kernel, pip, and bits of grit.

Like the gingerbread-and-gumdrop castles
we constructed on that table,
she is made to be consumed.
We delight her with our hearty appetites.

As sunflower, amaranth, millet, and rye
continue to flow, we understand at last
the task our mother, a horn of plenty,
sets before us:

to become like the birds—
lighter in bone, agile in air,
able to digest the small
persistent stones of her loss.

Remains in Our Days

Judith Yarrow
for Barbara

Where is she now?
Mostly ashes,
dispersed gases,
memory? Memory.

Thoughts of her
rattle in us,
raise questions.
Come to no answer,

or come to an answer
we don't want, can't
avoid. She passes.
Only her thoughts remain,

sinking deeper into us.
They simmer, flavor
our years, spice our lives,
meld into our thoughts.

We think them our own.
Remembered or not,
she still shapes us,
speaking through our lips.

If Winter Promises

JUDITH YARROW

I lie here in an age-worn body,
still piecing together mosaics
from the broken dreams I've followed
on my way to this dark night.

Winter keeps rolling through my life.
Its arrival unpredictable but certain.
Outward forms die. The juice is gone,
empty thoughts rattle aimlessly

inside this dry husk. A strong wind
could swirl me away. All becomes quiet.
Grows dense. Sinks inward.
Stirs.
       I know it will stir.

After the last hope has frozen solid
and shattered, spring, as unpredictable
as winter and as certain in the cold night,
will unfold, and the juice will rise.

My Mother's Hair

KATHLEEN WEDL

My hair are so terrible
she complains, using the plural
as if each strand hangs guilty.

Her hairdo is eighty years strong
judging from photos of these finger
waves set into the top of her head, fluted

like pie crust. She keeps a rake behind the door
to smooth vacuum cleaner tracks, ironing board
ready should a wrinkle arise. Beware the bathroom

where Aqua Net hairspray lingers, laminates tonsils—
the spray can— a lasso she twirls, rounding up loose ends,
a refinement rodeo.

Before Calling the Coroner

KATHLEEN WEDL

While my skin still clings, dress me in silk,
   anoint my lips with scotch.

Parade me with a jazz band, costumed children,
   pigs in tutus, family clowns.

Chop me up and place me on a mountain top.
   Let the vultures feast.

Burn me inside the belly of a bull
   as the dragon stands witness.

Bury me in a hollowed-out tree trunk
   or beneath the kitchen table.

Exhume my body later, spray it with wine
   and let the band play.

Dance my essence slow and sexy.
   Send me off with the song of laughter.

If a coffin it must be, make it a Lamborghini
   or a warm mixed-berry pie.

More Time

ELIZABETH BRULÉ FARRELL

I thought I had more time,
perhaps I did not appreciate
that beauty was fleeting.
Every day I passed the azalea
in the driveway, steadfast
through the seasons. Finally
when it blossomed I was
thrilled, cutting tender limbs,
arranging them in glass vases.
Then the unexpected storm.
The flowers were done.
Had I anticipated the weather
I might have filled my arms
with one more bouquet.
Or maybe not.

Mending

ELIZABETH BRULÉ FARRELL

He wakes up and wants an apple pie.
Over breakfast coffee it is decided
we will make one. His hands do not
hurt when holding the knife, so he peels
the red skins onto the counter. We work
while the morning energy is with me.
As my floured fingers place the top layer
over the fruit, it tears. Tenderly I gather
the edges, patch together a new pattern.

The Art of Chickens

JOANNE M. CLARKSON

for Veronika

The work saved her: little orchard
and a shack full of chickens. Hands plunged
into the shifting corn. Spring
with its broods of black-and-yellow
peeps. Her husband

was cruel. Her life gnawed by debt, the wailing
of children, five-to-a-bed. I slept
next to her one summer, braiding
white hair with five-year-old fingers,
oldest son's child, his father's hazel eyes
made kind. Her able fingers

kneaded over mine to form dumplings, fat noodles
draped over clotheslines to dry. She placed within
my tongue the Slovak names for cherries
and plums. One afternoon,

I found a snakeskin in hen house rafters,
evidence of how a body steps out of a body, swings
the ghost of a noose while venom slithers away.
Her secret was to raise

more chickens than serpents, more fruit
than bruises. To catch from the corner of her eye,
the flick of a tongue, and snatch
just in time, the fragile shell, shadow
of a pulse within.

Salt and Silver

JOANNE M. CLARKSON

Like a woman glancing over her left
shoulder, the bowl of the found spoon
is twisted. Dowry of the seashore
at my feet today. So much of any beach
is salvage. The finish is remarkably
untarnished, pitted gently by the pulse
of salt. I shudder as a thread runs
from my palm to a lost home: broth
or ice between chapped lips.
A darkened room. Crooning.

She is feeding her mother. Silver
roses the emblem between them.
How many holidays to the right of a plate?
Some curves endure beyond
the body. Some makeshift mirrors.
The vision is gone with a wind shift
and I am left with a glimpse
of my own mother, a feast
of emptiness. Relic of place
handed down over water, woman
to woman, spoon by spoon.

To My Thirties

SUSAN MICHELE CORONEL

I didn't swallow your sand and soil
when time pimpled days with feathers,
nor succumb to the weighty rush that wends

days into weeks, weeks into years.
You offered the promise of more,
heft of ribcage and radish

amid the changeability of water.
With you, I donned the second skin
of youth, turned pages of picture books,

rocked babies with the ease of song.
I preferred you, sandwiched between
the turbulent twenties and faithless forties,

the language of cotton and napping,
savored sweet childhood dollops
and new friendships. How you matched

me with other families with children,
connections made as easily as breathing.
We tugged on lawns and blankets,

hugging and yawning, taking photos,
riding wind. Now my bones
no longer grow and muscles ache,

the path ahead sliced at sharper
angles. Sometimes I miss you,
look for wild horses in a land

that's no longer wild. You gave me
the fullness of family before
it dissolved like a sugar cube in tea.

To my thirties and the brocade of birth,
flashes of nipples sought and sweet fingers
received in mouth, grasping adult hands.

Dear Grief,

SUSAN MICHELE CORONEL

You're so thirsty for the past,
you make your prayers
sound like a swarm of hornets,

rainbow glass in my gut,
the crunch of gravel underfoot
where sad wives walk.

The whitewashed walls know you,
sense the thinning blood of time.
You're unquenchable, not for water

but for bone dry wine. Face to face
with you, I'm a coward in a clown suit
who recalls the lapsed chord,

the bare belly, capsized coin.
Why do you triumph when my outsides
are pushed in, my insides positioned

further away from life's joys—
mint, the lull of babies' laughter,
ridiculous stars? You put your finger

Dear Grief,

on the egg in the sky because it's fractured.
I want to be washed into lightness
but all I can do is sense gravity's slip,

wonder at the aching silver
of what's lost, the frayed summer,
tiny fish teeth persistent in the dark.

How Do I Look?

Rosanne Ehrlich

When I was nine I was invincible.
I could do anything,
sing any tune, run any race
and fly in my dreams,
how I looked was not a care
I was ready to take any dare.

Then I was too fat,
too tall, too homely, too ugly.
It was painful walking around
in the "wrong" coat,
the one I'd had to have but now hated.
I was thirteen.

Boys, Cars and Rock and Roll
high school somehow
showed me the code.
It was stiff petticoats beneath
circle skirts that swayed
when we did the Lindy.

At a college without distractions
now it was all about smarts
and I was doing the looking

How Do I Look?

watching classmates from everywhere
while avoiding frat boys' observations

At the business table
my distracted gaze was on
clothing other women were wearing
messages as to who they are.
(Ferragamo made the shoes to wear
Louis Vuitton were the bags to bear.)

Now pregnant and amused that
small breasts blown up
catch attention from the men
walking towards me on the sidewalk.
Then birth, while turned
inside out for all to look
but unimportant
when tasked with bearing pain.

And not so long ago
looking in the bathroom mirror,
the perfect angle
to count the little white hairs
above my upper lip and
frown at my sagging skin.

Now? I try to remember
why it mattered.

Sistine Skin

SHIRLEY FESSEL

Anyway last week
She heaved at leaving.
I'm so used to her,
I won't know how to
Let her go.

If I wanted to run
She would run.
If I wanted a child
She made me one.

I'm spoiled since
Most of the time
She didn't ask for
Anything special.

A meal, water and a minimum-
Air, automatic lungs
Hands that did my work.
Feet that supported me.

Eyes to channel beauty
Nostrils to enjoy flowers.
Lips that felt caress, even
Those tingled with music.

Yesterday she started
Resisting. She's become more
Demanding, asked for more
Accommodations.

Still overall my
Faithful companion.
I've criticized her
Unfairly, thoughtlessly.

Considering her burden,
I've become the burden,
She doesn't want to, can't
Carry anymore.

She's protected and exposed me.
This morning she reminded me
I will shift my shape soon,
Imagine another expression.

I can't.
          Now I must.
She's not asking nicely,
Calling the shots.

Will I miss her earthly disguise,
Letting my soul breathe?

Make Hay While . . .

D. DINA FRIEDMAN

There's a line at the edge
where they didn't cut,

the shape of the curve
a symbol of infinity,

as if someone might have the courage to ask
how many blades?

How many hairs on the dog
who salivates at the window,

nose primed for woodchucks
in the next available hole?

Deep in those uncountable hairs,
ticks lay eggs. I sit

at the window. The rain says,
pay attention. Make each breath count. I don't

count blades, or hairs, each season's
ruthless sprint to the next. Tomorrow, sharp grass

will dry in the sun. The dog licks my knee
with his insistent tongue. In the mirror,

strands of silver grass in my hair
worry lines seeded in skin.

The Trip

D. Dina Friedman

Can't stop for daydreams, I'll miss the plane.
Check for passport: sleeping
against skin. Car keys?
In the ignition. Silly me.
Whatever I've forgotten
we're going to a civilized country
known for ruins, very old bones.
No one will card me. Who cares
if I drink? Old folks are never naughty.
But I'm not old. Look at my crazy
joie de vivre, my supple skin.
The treadmill at the airport propels us
to the gate. If the plane doesn't crash,
it will metaphorically. Each moment
another scrapped chance to do differently,
with or without passport or keys.
Years before I turned matronly
I once found the keys in the freezer.
Yield to the brain's urge to wander
Or desire to restrain life's unfurling inevitability?
Can the wisdom of bones salve
slipping memory when I'm so tired,
my keys lost, my passport,
snug against my womb, expired.

Hellcat, Witch or Crone

ERICA KENT

Personally, you favor Hellcat.
Hellcat dodges flames,
fur unsinged.
Or Witch might be better,
given how you cackle
at certain things.
As in, blood's done.
Babies go away.
Parents shrink.
Even so, your great, Crone heart
beats its offbeat beat
in free-form
rhapsody.

In truth, it's debatable
whether you're wise
or just bitter
in a calm way.
Your life's an old dog.
You pet it,
even when it growls
at your persistent hand.
You pet it,
confess you love it,
and it believes you.

when I was just a girl

KATHLEEN HELLEN

I did not think
myself a forest
the roots
under my feet
invisible creation
I wrote the same poem
over over, twirling
sounds like pearls
when I was just a girl
I did not think
myself the rain
subtle gases
I did not think
myself a benefactress
I hid inside the hut
of breasts
the arch of thighs
Toms peeped
though inattentive
like effigies in wig
and paint who failed
castration. Their
name was Action
when I was just a girl

This Old Woman

RUSS ALLISON LOAR

Standing in line at the market
She nearly drops her cane
Searching her purse for a coupon,
For her money,
Checking a wrinkled list.

She tilts perilously,
Forgetting to balance herself,
Nervous because she is the next to pay.

This old woman stands
Next to the magazines,
Glossy young women
Ripe for mating.
Everywhere this old woman goes
The young world surrounds,
Confounds,
Reminds her how long it has been
Since desire.

We turn our eyes away,
Pretending not to notice
As she questions the cashier needlessly,
Counts out nickels and pennies,
Drawing out this time of human contact.

She places the coins in the cashier's hand,
Feels a radiant warmth from his skin.
It startles,
Her hand jerks
And three pennies fall to the counter,
Roll off the edge and are gone.

Her Last Day

RUSS ALLISON LOAR

I keep thinking about the last day I saw her alive,
Wanting to go back and change it,
Change myself,
Be more patient,
Less inclined to bolt and run from that nursing home,
Its cold linoleum floors and distracted nurses
Too busy to pay much attention to a dying old lady.
They were all dying there.

Oh yes, I knew she was dying,
But she'd been dying for years,
Dying slow.
I didn't realize death was so near,
A day away,
When she said:
"I've lived about as long as anyone has a right to live."

A single clear sentence
Rising above an hour of erratic thoughts.

Her room was too hot and stuffy that summer afternoon,
Magnifying the sickening concoction of antiseptics,
Damp bedding,
Decaying flesh,
Every room infused.

A ceiling-high television with painfully exaggerated colors
Was worrying her about the news,
Danger right there inside her room,
Inside her mind,
The world in flames.

I ached for escape.

I listened for the end of another incoherent sentence,
Locked eyes with my wife sitting across the tiny room,
Then signaled by rolling my eyes toward heaven.

"I've got to get going," I announced,
Seeing no end to her disjointed talk,
Needing refuge.

I did not return the next day,
A small vacation from the dreadful daily routine
So many months in the making.
The phone rang late,
Those unspeakable words,
Asking if I wanted to see her
Before her body was taken away.

In that dark and noiseless night
I wondered:
Had she seen me roll my eyes?
Taken it as a cue somehow?
Had I weakened her with my impatience?
Pushed her toward the inevitable?

The final few days are not the life,
I keep telling myself,
Not even the final few years.
The whole is what must be measured.
But oh dear God,
If I could just go back,
Change that one single day.

Legacy

PAM McALLISTER

"Look, sunbeams!"
you cooed, lifting my plump hands
to golden specks of dust,
establishing a habit of awe.

"Listen, poetry!"
Sunlight warms your gnarled fingers.
I read aloud words you can no longer see.
Now and then you forget my name,
but when I pause after *"The quality of mercy,"*
you continue matter-of-factly,
"is not strained."

Cultivating Rough Edges

PAM MCALLISTER

I want a life
like an old oak table
where friends gather
to exchange recipes and tell stories;
a table scarred and scuffed from use,
rough edges showing through,
where big-bosomed women
rest plump elbows and laugh.

Save me from Formica and stainless steel,
hard surfaces,
sleek, shiny, wiped clean, erased,
a Botoxed life.

Let my days
be like my grandma's kitchen table,
marred by scorch marks
from nights when things got too hot,
and stained with tears
from times they spilled over
right in the middle of everything,
but polished with love,
polished with love.

Crone

EILEEN MOELLER

1.
The body is on fire,
pain radiating from
its signal places.

She would give it
away if she could,
like a red flower, clipped
from the garden, but
who would take it?

She pictures a blue-faced
God, holding a newly lit match.

2.
The soul lives in a woman's belly
most of the time, like a tongue of fire.
Her thoughts are its children, fueling
her forward, helping her to hatch
from the imprisoning egg, to be
naughty sometimes, to be surprising.
A woman burns hotter than she looks,
and her belly grows bigger every year.

3.
She used to be a rabbit,
but now she's become a hawk,
winging out of herself, tired of hiding.

She used to feel like screaming
her truth to the world, but now
she's calmer, less like a mill race,
more of a wind climbing.

She wears her inner predator
on her sleeve, fishes for nourishment
with talons and eager beak.

The Prayers of The Body

EILEEN MOELLER

dance like tiny men
around and around
an elliptical halo
above her head.

Two times a baby came to her,
a little ark, on her waters.
Two times a solid wiggly child
to nurse and send full sail
into the fight for survival.

Now her womb sputters out
its last red words
in chunks, that spill
and slap against porcelain,
thick, fibrous, decaying:
her fertility soon to be silenced.

She's made herself an amulet,
hung it between her breasts,
to ward off the aches
and pains, to help her
wield the crone's ax.

She looks forward to going hollow,
filling up with ghost towns,
wasp nests, milkweed pods.

But for now, prayers fly
from her fingertips
like seeds on the wind.

The universe is contained
in a finite number of heartbeats,
and knowing this, spins her
dervish-beautiful as she sings.

The Birthday Fairy

MEREDITH TREDE

She called to me from the checkout counter,
a tiny lavender sprite, just the thing
to add to my daughter's birthday present.

I thought of the sprite as a thing until
last night, when my daughter told me she'd place
the fairy on her night table, and how

every morning the little creature had
moved. Her logical son said that wasn't
possible, until he saw it himself

and asked, *Is Grandma a Witch?* He'd been told
about my lifting his infant mother
out of her crib, just before the ceiling

collapsed; my knowing when unexpected
deaths would come to the family; and how my
Dad's newly dead appeared and spoke with him.

When I couldn't discern what would surely
be, from anxiety, I spurned foresight.
May this spirit keep watch over my child.

Last Laughs with The Banger Sisters

MEREDITH TREDE

Merry (me), Suzy (you), in this poem, and back in the day.
Hawn and Sarandon, groupie-sisters on the DVD.

Watching them, and watching you in the infusion-chair,
red hair spiraling back, laughing, crying, hooting.

They reminisce over a collection of Polaroids,
the penises of musicians and roadies they knew.

We never liked each other's boyfriends, and wonder
why keeping or losing virginity defined our sex lives.

You were warned, *Stay away. She's one of those beatniks.*
Polaroid: You: madras, penny loafers. Me: black, sandals.

Do it true, the movie daughter concludes, as did you.
I know you knew how much I loved you, still do.

The oncology nurse shushes us to remember that chemo
patients need quiet; we choke to not laugh again.

I flew home, promising to come back soon.
Three days later you died. I came back to eulogize.

So:
A Jewish redhead and a brunette Irish Catholic walk into a bar . . .

to live

THERESA W. PAULSRUD

without time and calm
creativity is not
retire to live

release

Theresa W. Paulsrud

ember burning hot
bound in amber gold regret
to be released how

Another Year

MARGE PIERCY

On my eighty-sixth birthday
I ponder my long past and short
future. What do I want to do
with light and life still open?

Ambition has flittered away.
I no longer expect recognition
my work deserves. No one's
going to give me free money.

I've worked from the time
I was twelve. I'll go on as
I can. Short projects now
I should be able to finish.

I will garden as long as I
can, will love my dear, enjoy
cats, friends, books, music.
I like to cook and write poetry.

I hope these pleasures
last as long as I do.

It Slowly Closes In

MARGE PIERCY

As I age, I grow shorter
skirts and pants grow longer.

As I age, sight and hearing
weaken, need grows stronger.

As I age, knees and back
complain ever more loudly

As I age, friends too weaken
and die. Must make more.

Tasks take twice as long
I get half as much done.

Age diminishes me but
could I really handle more?

To still be alive is surprising.
Relish each minute left.

There's Madness in My Family

WENDY TIGERMAN

There's madness in my family
People who completely lose touch with reality

My cousin Molly walks around in mu-mus, flip-flops and dirty
feet
She has long thick hairs growing out of her chin and her toes
There's dog shit all over her asphalt yard. And fucking yappy
dogs
Cousin Susan with her Joker smile, lives at home with her slack-
jawed sleep-walking mother -- both unemployed for decades
They're all in a trance
No one will look you straight in the eye
Cousin Barbara unloads paranoid anger like a meth-fueled
firing squad
Her homophobic brother Ron cracks, "Just kidding," after he's
assaulted you with darts dipped in his own fetid piss that he
keeps in jars along one wall of his Lakewood ranch-style house

Maybe it's not madness
Maybe it's just a strong identification with trailer trash or reality
TV
Whatever it is, I'm terrified

I'm six
Dad yanks me out of the pepper tree and pushes me through
the front door into our family matriarch's East Hollywood
living room
She's wearing her Sunday floral housedress and apron
Even though her legs are wrapped in thick beige hose, her
calloused toes are poking through ratty slippers
There's a boiled cow tongue on the kitchen counter
I flash on a half-squished water bug still wiggling on the
linoleum
Petie, grandma's canary, is singing in his cage
He doesn't know that this place is the breeding ground for
madness,
Mother's nest-full of dripping pods
Maybe that's because grandma hasn't killed grandpa yet, nor
has she begun the non-stop shoving of her false teeth in and
out of her mouth

Now her lips look like anemic earthworms. There's always
spittle in the corners of her mouth
She covers me with a wet juicy one
and the canary inside of me drops dead

Two of a Kind

WENDY TIGERMAN

I wonder if my Great Aunt Sophie died happy
My mom didn't like her
No filter
Dangerous spontaneity
Lipstick on her teeth

One time she stirred her steaming hot coffee
Then pressed the sterling silver spoon on my mother's wrist
Not funny
Not funny at all

But to me, she was always
Loving
Devoted
Silly
Generous

Sophie was kicked out of her family for loving a Black man
She was an entrepreneur in Downtown L.A. before women had
the right to vote

She wore a visor to fancy dinners at Lawry's
with a transistor radio tuned to KFI, plugged in her ear

At the Park La Brea she had one room filled with Dodgers'
programs
Box scores neatly and carefully filled out
My dad introduced her to Vin Scully up in the broadcast booth
And she was buried along with a baseball autographed by Sandy
Koufax

I wonder if her friends ever got fed up
Barely tolerated her
Whether her children hated her
Did others even know her sweetness and loyalty?

Seduced by extremes
I am my Aunt Sophie
And probably the only one who misses her still

Awaken

Jo-Ann Vega
Dedicated to Dr. Clarissa Pinkola Estés,
author of *Women Who Run With the Wolves*

Forgive yourself for being human
having made mistakes and
stoked needless suffering
Bear witness and express gratitude
for the transformation wrought
by a half century or more of
B E I N G

Recognize the new unfamiliar countenance
in the mirror, a survivor, adapter,
in tune with and accepting of personal history
No longer willing to silently
bear the burden of the impossible
or choke down feelings and opinions
The time to sacrifice self and play games is past
Elevate the background and celebrate resilience

Accept the invitation
to awaken to the crone within,
acutely sensitive to the callings of
La loba, the wolf woman,
collector of the indestructible bones,
knowings outside of time
You've already been initiated

Resist the temptation to abandon the field
you have prepared and tended
Embrace the opportunity rather than lament the effort
Listen to the fatigue and need for renewal
Be alert to signs of your life force returning
Awaken and step into yourself with hope
Now exhale, get up, and
stay on the path

Limbo

NANCY SHIFFRIN

a Hebrew word for purgatory
the space between lives
where sins are purged and the next tasks defined
shame reduced blame disappeared
and all forgiveness possible
what happens there
what book is written

I know how to live there
shrouded unable to pull the trigger
pretending joy at the border
the place where you can't forgive yourself
and the god's forgiveness isn't enough
Limbo I know you
I've done that back bend under the wire

old age once a hopeless state of waiting to die
defined by a magazine as fifty
at fifty I received my phd
became a great aunt
experienced menopause

at 76 still birthing new poems

A Child is Born

NANCY SHIFFRIN

a miracle
three wise men look to the heavens
see this infant
born to a woman free of sin
a man probably not his biological father
willing to nurture him
we are asked to believe the mother was virgin
touched by an angel inseminated by god
she nursed the infant
cleaned his shit wiped snot from his nose

the boy will evict the money-changers
cure the sick raise the dead
embrace the prostitute forgive his betrayer
ascend the cross welcome
the nails pounded into his palm
he will be cared for in caves
resurrected to return as Holy Ghost
to say we are One in god's name

with children I love
I've hiked the back trail to Griffith Park Observatory
read *Goodnight Moon* and *Goosebumps*
listened to critiques of

One Fish Two Fish The Emperor's New Clothes
at Palisades Park we ride the Ferris Wheel
marvel at the wide sweep of the bay
dolphins playing we explore the Arcade
delight in the slinky toy won as a prize

we commemorate Christ's birth
with song and story ornaments and presents
each child a gift each with a message
a new set of trials

The Dark Queen

LAURENCE SNYDAL

Don't ask what beauty buys. It is a gift
That cripples. Turn your own dark eyes away
From what mine saw. I wakened to a day
I never wanted. In my glass, I shift
And shudder and I watch the shadows drift
To darkness. All I knew of beauty lay
Within those shadows and their will to stay.
The dwarves meant nothing. None I knew could lift
Life high enough to look again through eyes
I'd envied and that whitened cheek was true
To death or sleep. I didn't know how wise
I was or weak. So really all I knew
Was that those eyes were shut. The mirror lies.
The truth: I did what beauty made me do.

Mad Meg (after Breughel)

LAURENCE SNYDAL

Mad Meg, with her fireman's black helm, her bag
Crammed with pan and pot under an armor shell,
Strides ungainly through shatter and shock, hag
And her plunder straight from the mouth of Hell.
The bashful demons of our deepest dreams
Hail her or on their own, wander bemused,
Lost in their world of weird. Somehow it seems
No creatures were more carefully abused.
Somehow this scene of horror doesn't fright.
So surreal and stricken is this city
That viewers' eyes don't flutter into flight
But gaze in glazed Socratic pity.
Even Hell gapes only for the dentist drill,
All unconcerned with anything but when.
No fiery flame disturbs him but he will
Undoubted welcome back Mad Meg again.

So will we all be welcomed down below
When demons and dementia make it so.

Making Up

Terri Watrous Berry

Woman! Please paint your naked
face, are you trying to scare
the world? Who are you to think
they are ready for the truth?
You did quite contently cover
dewy youth's bloom on your cheek,
now when fairly reeking
with the silent scent of age,
you propose to pose
unmasked and unadorned?

Yes oh holy yes and for the rest of
all my days, for they are just mine,
and I choose to feel the sunshine
on my own and lonely skin, if
you cannot see fit to see me
as I am then look away!
Until the day a stranger touches
blush to ghastly gray, and
plays with hues on lips of blue—
will they be blue enough for you?

And Puppy Dog Tails

Terri Watrous Berry

The amber in her tresses fades
daily to white, causing her to wonder
if she will resemble a skunk,
after all the locks from yesterdays

dyes have been snipped, half and
half now—half what is real, half
the false color she had felt
made her presentable to the world.

Friends gasp, ask why look old?
She smiles and knows she looks
no older than she is, but
gazing in the glass she sees

a skunk to be the wrong simile.
Rather she thinks of a wriggly snake,
fresh from a worn-out skin, and of
butterflies aloft upon their first wind.

The Other

ALISON STONE

I have never been the perky sister, never danced
with clean-cut boys in high school gyms.
My fur coat and yearning led me elsewhere.
Hauled off to a judge's chamber, I'd confess
I never learned to purr,
but howl to my kin as daylight dies,
my nightshade heart tuned to the moon.
Prey safe for now in their dens.
The sky confettied with stars.

For My Aunt, Recovering

Alison Stone

Ram Dass said he'd been *stroked*,
as though God had reached down
to gently touch his cheek. I don't know
what deities do with their hands
but would grant angel status
to the phone friend who, alarmed
by your garbled words, called 911.
Two years of pandemic loneliness
and CNN would raise anyone's blood pressure.
Something, fortunately small, inside you
broke. As revelers drank and balls dropped
welcoming a new and hopefully-better year,
we waited. Your mother and my mother
dead, you're the family matriarch.
Was it that responsibility or your daughter,
holding vigil by the bed, that reached you?
Some divinity or luck returned you to us,
though with the salty coarseness
of your fishmonger father and Yiddish-
cursing mom. You sat up, spat out,
Fuck all of this shit,
and then your speech came back.

Night Keepers

LINDA STREVER

1714, Schoharie Creek Valley, Colonial New York

The others spoke of them with fearsome words, as if
    the noises of darkness were curses or slanders
    put forth by the land. Yet the beings of the dark
    did their nightly work. Agnes knew this to be true.

Oma had taught her the symmetry of opposites, of moon
    and sun, winter and summer, east and west, of all
    partnered forces woven together to make the world.

She recounted old tales of wolves with the power of speech
    and she-bears who mothered lost children. *The men*
    fear them needless, she would say. *They know not*
    their protection. Wolf and Bear be keepers of night.

Oma's eyes shone with remembrance, as she told the story
    of the girl who lost her way in the forest at day's end.
    Her basket of berries was heavy, and she stumbled
    over rock and root. The air grew chill and dank.

Then a she-bear come and wrap her in her arms, same
    as I hold ye now, Oma said, *and she slept warm*
    all the night. She-Bear guard children, always.

In the new land, the others could abide neither darkness
   nor forest. But Agnes bid welcome to both,
   as vital as luminous day and neatly tilled field.

The singing of wolves was a comfort. *If they take a sheep,
   it be needful*, she thought. But it did no good
   to speak of it. The minds of the others were hard.

On washing day, at the edge of the creek, she came upon
   bear tracks glistening in the mud. Agnes placed
   a small water-worn stone in each of the prints,
   for the little babe who was growing inside her.

"Oma" is German for "grandmother"

I wear scars on the inside

JC SULZENKO

Butt ugly, though perhaps not to Henry Moore. Had he used
a peephole to spy on women under showers in the locker room,
he'd have found inspiration enough to fill two great galleries
with merciless reveals, aging bodies rendered in bronze or stone.

His rough surfaces, awkward bulges and folds celebrate lost
elasticity, flesh rippled and stippled as it droops from breasts and
stomachs, hips, and thighs. Gravity, no friend to women, plays with
form, puckers skin abandoned by hormones that kept bodies firm,
beautiful each in its own way.

Today, the women soap and slip arthritic hands over layers of fat
that tell tales. One grand dame a cartoonist wouldn't dare portray
or risk censure stands unbothered by her seersucker skin. Her belly,
her haunches balloon and bunch like harem pants. If I ever look
like that, I'll hide myself away.

Later, her bulk enveloped by towels, she caresses each foot
with pearly cream. Size 6, at most. Dainty. When the cocoon
slips off her shoulders, her narrow back emerges—skin rosy,
smooth as a newborn's. I turn away, ask myself who is the fairer.

Do-si-do

JC SULZENKO

Behind the palisade next door—
high cedar planks and a locked gate—
a woman promenades through primroses
Ghost beauty haunts her eyes
Cloud-white hair, swept up, frames her face

She holds her head high as a princess
from an ancient regime
who wears only silks in shades of aquamarine
She once pitched her canvases in drawing rooms
With brush and palette, caught her subjects lives
between the lines of their skin

Now her paintings lounge along corridors
like a chorus line in the wings
She uses an umbrella to walk
Pokes people with it for attention
Giggles and asks if she's lost her teeth—
they're loose but still there
She's outrageous 'friends' whisper behind her back

I back away from their disdain
Remember her lovely, commanding an audience
When I next see her, she smiles

I can't remember all the names . . .
Doesn't remember mine, a friend of forty years
When she turns her back to me
as if I wasn't there, I turn from her
for the first time

Grandmother's Button Box

ERIC MACHAN HOWD

"My mother's in there,"
she said while mending my shirt,
never once lifting her eyes
from her work. I stared,
admiring the royal blue
porcelain horse set
into the small lid,
how the silver trim
hung in her eyes,
the cotton light
of her work lamp.

"All her recipes,
painting, songs, poems,
they're in there."

Late one night
while she slept,
I crept into her sewing room
and opened the box;
it was empty.

Of Icons & Other Things

BONNILEE KAUFMAN

Dedicated to Quentin Crisp & Oliver Sacks

I try to believe
anything
can be stored forever
in sealed containers. Lavender oil safe.
So what if that's an illusion?
My style of meditation
one-dimensional
ignores what I can't see
the rounded back poor posture
worsening.

Sometimes I breathe breath enough
to fill the void, watch windows grow steamy
lured by envy & the surface of things
the way green moss hugs a rock.

There is no point, having a piano if your fingers ache.

I want to transform
become a mini-icon, a Quentina Crispah. Expand
my circle, publish, orate & begin to love. Again
so sick of peanut butter
jelly & going to bed sticky.

What is the point of reminiscing about the time
milk bottles delivered at dawn, gathered
from stoops, not a drop wasted
rinse & return. Then plastic bloomed. Wild.
Took over landscapes
pernicious as tumbleweeds, there are people like that
scare me.

Glitzy gym-toned high-lifers, I've experienced none.
Everybody brushes past. Me
one of those aging queers
drenched in mentholated muscle spasms
like something wished for
patches of pink scalp keep widening
unsightly as the used-to-be fashionable olive-green poncho
slips off in public
without her
to lean against.

I am not sure what happened. But every time I open the fridge
something stinks. And lately, it takes enormous effort just to get
up (or down) a flight of stairs. Out of bed.

Competition Amongst Old Friends

Bonnilee Kaufman

She said: You're not gonna believe this, I broke my ankle

I said: Well, you're not gonna believe this, I broke my arm

Score: 1:1 Even

Right outside the doctor's office, she explains. Already had the doctor appointment. Was on my way back home.

I reply, almost bored from hearing my rendition repeated so many times, fell in my very own apartment just like that pathetic old lady channel 11 commercial on TV. And yes, don't remind me, I was all alone. Arms flailing like the wings of a baby bird prematurely airborne. I witnessed every second of that slow descent. Heard the crack.

Score: 1:2 My Favor

Well, she said, turned blue & green & yellow & purple from the ankle, all the way up to. . . . winning colors.

Score: Even 2:2

Then she added the clincher; a really good friend came to visit
all the way from Tennessee (if he's such a good friend, how is it I
never heard of him before?). She was taking him to her favorite
hairstylist. Running late (this was before the whole ankle thing).
Backing the car out the driveway while Tennessee diddled with
the unwieldy gate. She drove right over his foot. Imagine that,
she said. You should've heard him.

Game over: She wins

About the Contributors

JENNIFER L. ABOD (www.jenniferabod.com) has a PhD in Intercultural Communication and Women's Studies. Her poetry appears in *Sinister Wisdom, One Art, Metro Washington Weekly*, and is forthcoming in *Artemis Journal*. She has presented poetry in Long Beach and Palm Springs, California, and at Outwrite 2022. Abod is an award-winning radio broadcaster, producer, talk-show host, and filmmaker. Her films include *The Passionate Pursuits of Angela Bowen, The Edge of Each Other's Battles: The Vision of Audre Lorde, Nice Chinese Girls Don't* (Women Make Movies), and *Look Us in the Eye: The Old Women's Project* (Terra Nova Films). She sang with the New Haven Women's Liberation Rock Band (1970-1976), and currently sings jazz at the restaurant Chez Bacchus.

TERRY A. ALLBRIGHT is a retired psychotherapist who specialized in trauma and disordered eating treatment. Before becoming a counselor, she worked as a high-risk labor and delivery nurse, parent educator, and nurse educator. She also taught behavioral medicine to internal medicine residents at the Texas Tech Health Sciences Center and is a contributor to the book, *Cinemeducation: A Comprehensive Guide to Using Film in Medical Education*. She recently finished the first of a three-part memoir series. She and her writer husband are delighted to live in Washington after many happy years in Texas.

JOAN ANNSFIRE is a retired librarian who lives in Berkeley. Her poetry chapbook, *Distant Music* was published by Headmistress Press. Her poetry has appeared in *Sinister Wisdom* (many issues), *Rising Phoenix Review, Birdland Journal, 11/9: The Fall of American Democracy, Older Queer Women: The Intimacy of Survival*, as well as *The Times They Were A-Changing: Women Remember the 60's and 70's*, *The Queer Collection, Milk and Honey: A Celebration of Jewish Lesbian Poetry*, *The Other Side of the Postcard*, Counterpunch's *Poet's Basement, Lavender Review, The 13th Moon, Bridges, The Evergreen Chronicles, The SoMa Literary Review*, and *The Harrington Lesbian Literary Quarterly*, among others. Visit annsfire.blogspot.com to discover more about her published work.

Carol Barrett coordinates the Creative Writing Certificate Program at Union Institute & University. She has published two volumes of poetry, including *Calling in the Bones*, which won the Snyder Prize from Ashland Poetry Press, and one volume of creative nonfiction, *Pansies*, a recent finalist for the Oregon Book Awards. A former NEA Fellow in Poetry, Carol has lived in nine states and in England. Her poems appear in such diverse journals as *JAMA, The Women's Review of Books, Nimrod, Poetry International*, and in over fifty anthologies. She holds doctorates in both Clinical Psychology and Creative Writing.

A Michigan septuagenarian, **Terri Watrous Berry**'s work has appeared over the past thirty-five years in anthologies, journals, magazines, and newspapers. In 2022 her poems were included in Wising Up's anthology *Adult Children*, House of Zolo's *Journal of Speculative Literature Vol. 3*, devoted to climate change, Oprelle's *Bigger Than Me* anthology on the subject of compulsion, *Syncopation Literary Journal*'s issue regarding age and change, University of Michigan Flint's *Qua Literary Journal*, the December issue of *Blink Ink*, and We'Moon's *Silver Lining*.

Stella Brice graduated from Rice University; and has worked, variously, as house cleaner, tarot reader and performance artist.

Her poems are published in journals and anthologies including *Southern Poetry Review, Word Riot, Right Hand Pointing, Gingerbread House, The Weight of Addition, Women. Period., Improbable Worlds,* and *No, Achilles.* She is a Pushcart and Best of the Net nominee; a winner of the John Z. Bennet Prize; and the author of five collections of poetry, including *Urged* and *Wait 'til I Get Fatter* (both by VAC/Purple Flag Press); and *Creatures* (INKira Press). Stella serves as a mentor and literary advisor for the PEN Prison Writing Program.

JEANNE BRYNER was born in Appalachia and her family was part of the outmigration. A retired emergency department nurse, she's a graduate of Trumbull Memorial Hospital School of Nursing and Kent State University's Honors College. She has several books in print. Her poetry has been adapted for the stage and performed nationally at the 2004 Fringe Festival of Edinburgh, Scotland. She has received writing fellowships from Bucknell, the Ohio Arts Council ('97, '07) and Vermont Studio Center. She lives with her husband near an Ohio dairy farm.

ANA MARÍA CARBONELL teaches literature and creative writing at Diablo Valley College in the Bay Area where she also serves as Co-Chair of the Literature and Creative Writing Committee. Her work has appeared or is forthcoming in *The MacGuffin, The Acentos Review, Mothers Always Write,* and The San Francisco Library Poem-a-Day Archive. One of her short stories was also a finalist for the Tucson Festival of Books Literary Competition. Ana María is the proud mother of two adult sons and lives in Berkeley, California, with her musician husband and their thriving rescue pup.

PHYLLIS CARITO is a poet, writer, and educator. She holds an MFA from Manhattanville College, Purchase, New York. A retired academic dean, she teaches creative writing through SUNY-CGCC. Her published writing includes the books: *barely a whisper*, *The Stability of Trees in the Winds of Grief*, *Worn Masks*, and a collaborative book, *Travel Light and Other Explorations*. Other work is included in: "Gathering Flowers: Living with the Death of a Child," *Passager Journal*, *Voices in Italian Americana*, *Fired Up!* (Berkshire Women's Writers), and *Trolley* NYS Writer's Institute. Her novel, *More Than Making Ends Meets* is being published by Bedazzled Ink, Inc.

SUSAN CAVANAUGH retired in 2020 from a thirty-year career in the health insurance industry, where she was an advocate for health care reform. This award-winning poet's early work appeared in *Yankee*, *Painted Bride Quarterly*, and *Smartish Pace*. Her chapbook, the *Good Sense of a Bird*, was published by Still Waters Press, Galloway, New Jersey. Cavanaugh's recent poems appear in *Common Ground Review*, *Oberon*, *Exit 13*, and *NJ Bards Poetry Review 2022*.

INDRA CHOPRA is a writer, researcher, and travel blogger (travtrails.com) from New Delhi, India. She holds a Masters in English Literature from Allahabad University, India. She began her writing career as a reporter with her hometown English daily. Stays in Sultanate of Oman, Hong Kong, and at present in Calgary, Canada, have widened her interests to travel writing and blogging, content writing, research for media documentaries, and women-centric short stories. She has contributed to *Femina*, *Woman's ERA*, *Pioneer* (India), *Khaleej Times*, *Times of Oman*, *Weekend* (Oman), *WIPS* (Hong Kong), and other publications. Her short stories have appeared in Indian and American anthologies.

JOANNE M. CLARKSON's sixth poetry collection, *Hospice House*, was published by MoonPath Press in 2023. Her poems have appeared in such journals as *Poetry Northwest, Nimrod, Poet Lore, American Journal of Nursing*, and *Beloit Poetry Journal*. She has received an Artist Trust Grant and an NEH grant to teach poetry in rural libraries. Clarkson has Master's degrees in English and Library Science, has taught and worked for many years as a professional librarian. After caring for her mother through a long illness, she re-careered as a registered nurse working in home health and hospice. See more at http://JoanneClarkson.com.

SUSAN MICHELE CORONEL's poems have appeared in numerous publications including *Spillway 29, TAB Journal, Inflectionist Review, Gyroscope Review, Prometheus Dreaming*, and *Thimble*. In 2021 one of her poems was runner-up for the Beacon Street Poetry Prize, and another was a finalist in the Millennium Writing Awards. She has received two Pushcart nominations. Her first full-length manuscript was a finalist in Harbor Editions' 2021 Laureate Prize. She has a M.S.Ed. in Applied Linguistics from the City University of New York and lives in Ridgewood, Queens, where she owns and directs a childcare business.

CARYN COYLE is an editor at the Baltimore based literary journal, *Loch Raven Review* and her work has appeared in more than four dozen literary publications. She has won awards for her fiction from the Maryland Writer's Association, the *New Millennium, Delmarva Review*, the Missouri Writer's Guild, the St. Louis Writer's Guild, and Pennsylvania's Hidden River Arts. She lives in Massachusetts.

ROSANNE EHRLICH's short pieces have been in *Chicken Soup for the Soul, Persimmon Tree*, and *Panoplazine. Fredericksburg Liter-*

ary Art Review, The Voices Project, and *True Grit Anthology* have published her poems, a non-fiction piece has appeared in *Metaphor Magazine* and her short stories have appeared in *Antirrhinum Journal,* Quillkeeper's Press' *Rearing in the Rearview,* and *Glitter Literary Journal.*

ELIZABETH BRULÉ FARRELL used to write advertising copy in Chicago before moving to southeastern Massachusetts. Her poems are published in the *Paterson Literary Review, Poetry East, Spillway, Pilgrimage, The Healing Muse, Earth's Daughters, Evening Street Review, The Comstock Review, Except for Love: New England Poets Inspired by Donald Hall, Unruly Catholic Feminists,* and other publications. She has been a recipient of The Louise Bogan Memorial Award for Poetry. She is truly glad to have her poems be a part of this anthology.

SHIRLEY FESSEL is a Midwest freelance writer in education and counseling. She earned a Master's in Communication and a Master's in Counseling from Wichita State University. Published in a variety of media, her interests are in the relationship of communication competency and mental health. *Evolving Magazine, Home Business, Northland Lifestyle,* and Park University have featured her writing. Her latest book was published in 2018: *Redemption from Biblical Battering,* a workbook for women whose faith is used against them to sanction their abuse. Visit her blog at ShirleyFessel.com or find her on Facebook or Twitter @fessup2.

SUZANNE FREEMAN is an internet-free vegan crone who draws inspiration from the written word and the natural world. Fiction and poetry credits include *Evening Street Review, Muse, Miramar,* and *Earth's Daughters.* Her dystopian novella, *Omnibo,* won the

214

Clay Reynolds Novella Prize and was published by Texas Review Press; her poetry chapbook, *The Sun's Banquet Table*, won the Orchard Street Press chapbook competition.

D. DINA FRIEDMAN's short story collection, *Immigrants*, is forthcoming from Creators Press in Fall 2023. She is also the author of one book of poetry, *Wolf in the Suitcase* (Finishing Line Press) and two young adult novels: *Escaping Into the Night* (Simon and Schuster) and *Playing Dad's Song* (Farrar, Straus and Giroux). Dina has published widely in literary journals and received two Pushcart Prize nominations.

GAY GUARD-CHAMBERLIN is a Chicago poet and artist. *Red Thread Through a Rusty Needle* (New Wind Publishing) is her first book of thirty-six poems. Gay often performs with her writer-sister, Anara Guard, as *Sibling Revelry: Two Sisters Reading Poetry*.

JOANN BREN GUERNSEY is the author of three young adult novels, several nonfiction books for middle-grade readers, anthologized short stories, the literary novel *Glass Asylum*, and the fiction chapbook *Tangled Strings*. In addition, she collaborated with Minnesota photographer and environmentalist Jim Brandenburg on four award-winning children's books. Her awards include the 2003 McKnight Artist Fellowship for Writers.

KARINE HALPERN has been producing creative content, as well as conducting independent, experimental, and innovative creative work in communications for several industries since 1990. Her focus has primarily been with the film and television industry. She is a member of a French writers' guild. With a Master's degree in Public and Political Communication and a Certificate in Cultural Mediation, she is now enrolled in a Transmedia PhD in Paris, France. In 2010, Karine founded Transmedia Ready, a think-and-do tank for creative projects, communication, and marketing campaigns with a transmedia strategy.

KATHLEEN HELLEN is an award-winning poet whose latest collection *Meet Me at the Bottom* was released in Fall 2022. Her credits include *The Only Country Was the Color of My Skin*, *Umberto's Night*, which won the poetry prize from Washington Writers' Publishing House, and two chapbooks, *The Girl Who Loved Mothra* and *Pentimento*. Featured on *Poetry Daily* and *Verse Daily*, Hellen's poems have won the Thomas Merton prize for Poetry of the Sacred and prizes from the *H.O.W. Journal* and *Washington Square Review*, as well as from the Maryland State Arts Council and Baltimore Office of Promotion & the Arts.

LENORE HIRSCH is a retired educator who lives in Napa Valley. She writes in many genres, including features in the *Napa Valley Register*, short stories, poetry, memoir, humor, and travel. She is a founding member of Napa Valley Writers, a branch of the California Writers' Club. Her books include her dog's memoir, *My Leash on Life: Foxy's View of the World from a Foot Off the Ground*; a poetry collection, *Leavings*; humorous essays, *Laugh and Live: Advice for Aging Boomers*; and a novel, *Schooled: Confessions of a Rookie Vice Principal*.

ANNE HOFLAND is an emerging writer who embraced writing later in life. She has published work in the *Existere Journal of Arts and Literature*, *Open Minds Quarterly*, and *Travel Scoop Magazine*, as well as three anthologies, *Breaking Boundaries* and Exisle Publishing's *Timeless Wisdom* volumes *Love & Loss* and *Fear & Courage*. She was a winner in the City of Toronto's "My City, My

Six" story competition, and earned honorable mention in the Ontario Poetry Society's Pandemic Poetry competition. Anne facilitates online expressive writing workshops with Expressive Arts Florida, and shares her time between Toronto, Florida, and northern Ontario.

ERIC MACHAN HOWD (Ithaca, New York) is a poet, musician, and educator. Their work has been seen in publications such as *River City, Nimrod, Slate, Caesura,* and *Stone Canoe.* Their fifth collection of poetry, *Universal Monsters,* was recently published by The Orchard Street Press. Their essay, "An Argument for a Non-Binary Approach to the Arts: the Continuum of Word and Song" was translated into Slovene and archived in the Slovenian National Library a few years ago. They are currently working on an erasure project using the work of author H.P. Lovecraft.

MIRIAM KARMEL's work has appeared in *Prairie Schooner, Alaska Quarterly Review, Calyx, Bellevue Literary Review, Water~Stone Review, Passages North, Moment Magazine,* and others. She is the author of the novel, *Being Esther* (Milkweed Editions, 2013), and a short story collection, *Subtle Variations and Other Stories* (Holy Cow! Press, 2017). She lives in Minneapolis.

BONNILEE KAUFMAN is a Lambda Literary Fellow, Queer-Wise emeritus, and aging femme. Her essays and poetry have recently appeared in *The Journal of Lesbian Studies, Not Like Any Other Fiction, Altadena Poetry Review,* and forthcoming in *42 Stories Anthology.* Her poetry was published in *Ghosts of the Holocaust, Milk & Honey: A Celebration of Jewish Lesbian Poetry, The Brillantina Project, Sinister Wisdom, Selfish, Gyroscope Review, Queer Loving Ang(st) Journal,* and the *Los Angeles Library Newsletter.*

ELIZABETH KENNEDAY, an Emeritá Professor of Art at the California State University in Long Beach, holds an MFA in Painting and Photography and a PhD in Critical Theory in Art from Claremont Graduate University. A Fulbright Scholar recipient at the University of Iceland, her activities in environmental education through art led to numerous lectures at international conferences. Her award-winning artworks, including a Julia Margaret Cameron Award, have been exhibited internationally. She has contributed chapters to several anthologies, and her book, *Regarding Mono Lake: Novelty and Delight at an Inland Sea,* received an Eric Hoffer Finalist Award.

ERICA KENT lives in Portland, Maine, with her family and chunky dogs. She's a devoted but irreverent high school English teacher and tutor. She holds an MFA from Vermont College of Fine Arts. Her work has been published in *StoryQuarterly, The Brooklyn Rail, The Offing,* and *The Maine Review,* among others.

NANCY KING writes, weaves, and hikes in Santa Fe, New Mexico. Her memoir, *Breaking the Silence* (Terra Nova Press) is available in paperback, ebook, and audiobook, online and in bookstores. Visit www.nancykingstories.com to read her monthly stories and world tales, discover excerpts of her memoir and novels, and learn about her work exploring the power of stories, imagination, and creativity, as well as find information about Nancy's workshops.

CONNIE LEVESQUE is a naturalist, writer, and gardener. She has an MFA in Creative Writing from Portland State University. Her work has appeared in *Wild in the City, The Cancer Poetry Project 2,* and the *Oregon Poetry Calendar, 2023.*

Russ Allison Loar's writing has appeared in the anthology *Heart of a Man, Bryant Literary Review, High Shelf Press, Bright Flash Literary Review, Oddball Magazine, Abstract Magazine, Evening Street Review, Wising Up Press* anthologies, *Coffin Bell Journal, Ravens Perch, Daring to Repair* anthology, *Poetry in the Cathedral* anthology and *Telling Our Stories Press* anthology. Loar has a degree in journalism and has written news and feature stories for newspapers including the *Los Angeles Times* under the byline: Russ Loar. Loar's photography is published worldwide, including: ABC News, PBS and NPR websites, City News Service and Yahoo! News.

Katharyn Howd Machan, author of forty collections of poetry (most recently *Dark Side of the Spoon* from Moonstone Press in 2022 and *A Slow Bottle of Wine*, winner of the Jessie Bryce Niles Chapbook Competition, from Comstock Writers, Inc. in 2020), has lived in Ithaca, New York, since 1975 and has taught Writing at Ithaca College since 1977. After many years of coordinating the Ithaca Community Poets and directing the national Feminist Women's Writing Workshops, Inc., she was selected to be Tompkins County's first poet laureate. Her poems have appeared in numerous magazines, anthologies, textbooks, and stage productions, and she has edited three thematic anthologies, most recently a tribute collection celebrating the inspiration of Adrienne Rich.

Ronna Magy is a poet, textbook author, and retired ESL instructor who holds a Master's in Social Welfare from UC Berkeley. She recently coordinated a reading of lesbian poets over sixty for the OutWrite Festival. Her poems have appeared in *Coal Literary Journal, Stone Poetry Quarterly, Persimmon Tree, Writing in a Woman's Voice, Writers Resist, Artists and Climate Change,*

American Writers Review, Sinister Wisdom, and *Nasty Women Poets*.

J.T. MARLOWE is a theatre practitioner and mindfulness educator (and minimalist) in Southern California.

LYNN MARTIN has appeared in *Calliope, South Florida Review, The Garden State, Sinister Wisdom, Earth's Daughters*, and a 2012 anthology: *New York City Bridges in Poetry*. She is a member of Write Action in Brattleboro, Vermont. She has four published books: *Visible Signs of Defiance, Talking to the Day, Birds of a Feather*, and *Living Diversity*. Visit lynnmartin.com for a complete biography.

PAM MCALLISTER's poems, articles, essays, and book reviews have been published in numerous anthologies, literary magazines, newspapers, and blogs. She is also the author of nonfiction books and plays. She clings to a countercultural life in a quiet, book-filled apartment in Brooklyn, the City That Never Sleeps within easy reach. Employed as a musician, Pam often writes Facebook posts celebrating feminism, nonviolent activism, courage, and creativity.

HILLORIE SUE MCLARTY is a memoirist, novelist, short story writer, and poet. She is a Los Angeles, California native, currently living in Nashville, Tennessee. She received her BA from New College, Cal State San Jose and her MA in English from Belmont University in 2022. She has begun a PhD program in English at Middle Tennessee State University. Hillorie is continually writing her story and would love to hear your story as well.

EILEEN MOELLER lives in southern New Jersey with her husband Charlie. She was born in 1950, and raised in Paterson, New Jersey. She's had poems in numerous literary journals and anthologies. Her books are *Firefly, Brightly Burning* (Grayson Books, 2015); *The Girls In Their Iron Shoes* (Finishing Line Press, 2017); *Silk City Sparrow* (Read Furiously Inc., 2020); and *Waterlings* (Cherry Grove Collections, 2023). Her blog: And So I Sing: Poems and Iconography is at https://eileenmoeller.blogspot.com.

ELAINE NAMANWORTH is a native New Yorker who is enjoying her retirement by eating too much chocolate and reading two randomly selected poems on a daily basis. Her poems have appeared in *Fine China: Twenty Years of Earth's Daughters, Anthology of Magazine Verse and Yearbook of American Poetry, Black Maria, City Magazine, Day Tonight/Night Today, Earth's Daughters #10-11,* and *The Helen Review.*

PENELOPE PAGE is a late bloomer in the field of writing. A writer's group helped turn her hobby into a full-time passion. She's written columns for three county newspapers, and several of her short stories appeared in a Wisconsin anthology. At seventy-one, she hopes to have her first novel, *Sleuths with Sticks,* published in 2023. She's honored the ladies at Wild Librarian Press found her little piece amusing.

THERESA W. PAULSRUD is a recently retired library administrator living in Southern California and mother of two. She is currently learning the pathways for becoming a suicide loss survivor.

Knopf published **MARGE PIERCY**'s twentieth poetry book *On the Way Out, Turn Off the Light* and previously published her *Made in Detroit.* She read the audiobook for *On the Way Out, Turn Off* *the Light*. PM Press reprinted three of her novels, published a collection of her short stories, *The Cost of Lunch, Etc.*, and published her essays and poems in *My Life, My Body*. Her memoir is *Sleeping with Cats*. Her most recent novel is *Sex Wars*. She has given readings, workshops, or speeches at more than 575 venues in the U.S. and abroad. She has been an activist on abortion and feminist causes since she was eighteen.

ANITA PINATTI is spending her retirement sending her poetry out there into the world of small-press publishers. Her poems have recently appeared in *Glimpse, The Comstock Review*, and *Visions International* and will be forthcoming in *SALT 5*.

NANCY WERKING POLING's work reflects her concern for women, racial justice, and the environment. Her published books include *White Earth Still Speaks*, a novel; *Before It Was Legal: A Black-White Marriage (1945-1987)*, non-fiction; *Had Eve Come First and Jonah Been a Woman*, a story collection; and *Out of the Pumpkin Shell*, a novel. Her essay, "Leander's Lies," won the 2018 Alex Albright Creative Non-fiction Award. She posts on Facebook and Instagram and blogs at nancy@nancypoling.com. She lives and writes in the North Carolina mountains.

SUZANNE RHODENBAUGH is the author of poetry books *The Girl Who Quit at Leviticus* (Homestead Lighthouse Press, 2022); *The Whole Shebang* (WordTech, 2010); *Lick of Sense* (Helicon Nine Editions, 2001), winner of the Marianne Moore Poetry Prize; four chapbooks; and the essay collection *The Deepest South I've Gotten* (Hell Yes Press, 2017). She lives in St. Louis.

CINDY RINNE (www.fiberverse.com), a Pushcart Award nominee, is a poet and fiber artist living in San Bernardino, California. She translates the world into an alternate reality of verbal mosaics. Cindy attended a residency at Desert Dairy Artist Residency. She performed "Dancing Through the Fire Door" during the Pacific Ancient and Modern Language Association conference at UCLA. Her poems appear in literary journals, anthologies, art exhibits, and dance performances. She is the author of *The Feather Ladder* (Picture Show Press), *Words Become Ashes: An Offering* (Bamboo Dart Press), *Today in the Forest* (Moonrise Press), and others. Her poetry has appeared in *The Closed Eye Open*, *Verse-Virtual*, *Mythos Magazine*, and other publications.

MARGARET M. RODEHEAVER writes short fiction and novels for children and adults, including *Porkington Hamm*, winner of a 2020 Georgia Independent Author of the Year Award. Her poetry has appeared in *Cricket Magazine*. Margaret enjoys music and travel and lives with her husband near Macon, Georgia. They share a cat with the neighbors. Find Margaret online at www.margaretrodeheaver.com.

NANCY SHIFFRIN is the author of four collections of poems: *The Vast Unknowing* (Infinity Publishing), *Game With Variations*, *Flight*, and *This Sacred Earth*. The poems appearing in this anthology are included in *This Sacred Earth*. *Flight* and *This Sacred Earth* were written after her 70th birthday. Her prose has appeared in the *Los Angeles Times*, *Shofar*, and *Outlook: Canada's Progressive Jewish Magazine*. More works are listed at www.NancyShiffrin.net. She lives in Santa Monica, California, with her husband, the novelist Thomas Page.

ELLEN SHRINER is one of the founders and contributors to the shared blog *WordSisters*. Her short memoirs have been published in several anthologies (*The Heart of All That Is: Reflections on*

Home, *Mourning Sickness*, and *It's About Time*). Her personal essays have appeared in *Tangled Locks*, *Medical Literary Messenger*, *The Sunlight Press*, *BREVITY's Nonfiction Blog*, *Wisconsin Review*, *Mothers Always Write*, *BrainChild*, and elsewhere. She lives in Minneapolis, Minnesota, with her husband, and she has two grown sons.

CLAUDETTE MORK SIGG received an MA in English Language Arts with an emphasis on Creative Writing from San Francisco State University. After a long teaching career, she retired and became an art, history, and natural sciences docent at the Oakland Museum of California. The OMCA has proved to be inspirational, and many of her poems were born out of museum experiences. Her work has appeared in publications such as *Natural Bridge*, *The Atlanta Review*, *The Comstock Review*, *Common Ground Review*, *Sierra Songs & Descants*, *The Journal of the American Medical Association*, *75 Poems on Retirement*, and *Cradle Song*.

LAURENCE SNYDAL is a poet, musician and retired teacher. He has published more than a hundred poems in magazines such as *The Cape Rock*, *Spillway*, *Columbia*, and *Steam Ticket*. His work has also appeared in many anthologies including *Visiting Frost*, *The Poets Grimm*, and *The Year's Best Fantasy and Horror*. Some of his poems have been performed in Baltimore and New York City. He lives in San Jose, California, with his wife Susan.

ALISON STONE has published eight full-length collections, including *To See What Rises* (CW Books, 2023), *Zombies at the Disco* (Jacar Press, 2019), *Caught in the Myth* (NYQ Books, 2019), *Dazzle* (Jacar Press, 2017), *Ordinary Magic* (NYQ Books, 2016), *Dangerous Enough* (Presa Press 2014), and *They Sing at Midnight*, which won the 2003 Many Mountains Moving Poetry Award; as well as three chapbooks. Her poems have appeared in *The Paris Review, Poetry, Ploughshares, Barrow Street, Poet Lore,* and others. She has been awarded *Poetry*'s Frederick Bock Prize and *New York Quarterly*'s Madeline Sadin Award. She is also a painter and the creator of The Stone Tarot (www.stonetarot.com). Visit www.stonepoetry.org to discover more.

LINDA STREVER is the author of *My Life in Cars* (poetry), *Against My Dreams* (poetry), and *Don't Look Away* (fiction). Her poetry has been published in numerous journals and anthologies. Winner of the Lois Cranston Memorial Poetry Prize and a Pushcart Prize nominee, her work has been a finalist for the New Issues Poetry Prize, the Levis Poetry Prize, the Ohio State University Press Award in Poetry, and the Eludia Award in fiction. She has an MFA from Brooklyn College, has worked as a proofreader, editor, graphic artist, teacher, trainer and mediator, and lives in the Pacific Northwest.

Canadian **JC SULZENKO**'s poetry appears in anthologies and journals in print and online, either under her name or as A. Garnett Weiss. Aeolus House published *Bricolage, A Gathering of Centos,* a finalist for the 2022 Fred Kerner Book Award from the Canadian Authors Association. Point Petre Publishing released *South Shore Suite . . . POEMS* (2017). JC has written six books for children and a play about dementia. She delivered workshops for the Ottawa International Writers Festival, Ottawa Public Library, and many school boards and Alzheimer societies. She selects for the online journal *Bywords* and founded and curated "Poetry Quarter" in the *Glebe Report.* She serves on the Executive Committee of the Ontario Poetry Society.

WENDY TIGERMAN, a mostly-retired copywriter, broadcast producer, and creative director, is a writer, photographer, and collage artist. She's a student of Tibetan Buddhism and an irreverent wisecracker. She gardens daily, talks to strangers, and pesters her rescue pooches for love. She takes photos constantly, writes irregularly, and creates award-winning collage. Wendy's proudest moment as a writer came when Allen Ginsberg told her husband that to be a better poet, he should walk around and write down *everything* she said. In her work, "first thought, best thought" guides her and she tries to write as she speaks. Her purpose in life is to be kind, generous and create beautiful moments. Visit www.wendytigerman.net to discover more.

MEREDITH TREDE (www.meredithtrede.com) is the author of three poetry collections: *Bringing Back the House*, *Tenement Threnody*, and *Field Theory*. A Toadlily Press founder, her chapbook, *Out of the Book*, was in *Desire Path*. Extensive journal publications include *Barrow Street*, *Feminist Wire*, *Friends Journal*, *Gargoyle*, *Gathering of Tribes*, and *The Paris Review*. She has held residencies at Blue Mountain Center, Ragdale, Saltonstall, and the Virginia Center for the Creative Arts in Virginia and France. Meredith has been a librarian, a teacher of French, Spanish, ESL, and writing. She lives in New York City.

A published author, and dynamic speaker with more than thirty years of experience presenting to academic, business, and community groups, **JO-ANN VEGA** lives with her life partner and canine companion. Jo-Ann's debut poetic memoir *Wolf Woman & Other Poems* (2022) received a Bronze Medal in the Poetry category in Reader Views Reviewer's Choice Awards, 2022-2023. Other recent publications include: *Moments in Flight: A Memoir* (2021); "Serendipity" and "Empathy in the Time of COVID"

(Volume 21 and Volume 22 of *Story Circle Network's Annual Real Women Write Anthology,* 2021-2022). Several poems published include: *Musings, Then & Now, Awaken,* and *In Remembrance.*

MARY VOLMER is the author of two novels: *Crown of Dust* (Soho Press, US) and *Reliance, Illinois* (Soho Press). Her essays, reviews, and short stories have appeared in *Mutha Magazine, Arc Digital, Fiction Writers Review, Historical Novel Society Review, The New Orleans Review, Brevity,* and *Ploughshares.* She has been awarded a Rotary Ambassadorial Scholarship, residencies at the Vermont Studio Center and Hedgebrook, and was a Distinguished Visiting Writer in Residence at Saint Mary's College, where she now teaches.

KATHLEEN WEDL is a life-long Minnesotan. During and since her fifty years as a nurse specializing in behavioral health, her writing has help bridge a gap in understanding herself and her world. Kathleen's poetry has been recognized in contests and journals. When not reading, writing, and enjoying nature, you may find her studying the pairings of good food and music, especially in the company of family and friends. Her debut poetry collection, *Ordinary Time,* was released in May 2023 by Kelsay Books.

RITA WILSON is an artist, writer, and educator. She has been published in wolfmatters.org, *Rune* and *Riverspeak* literary magazines, *Voices from the Attic,* and the *100 Lives Anthology.* Her biography/memoir, *Greek Lessons* was published in 2016. Wilson earned her MFA in Creative Non-Fiction from Carlow University. A retired teacher, she continues to teach creative and professional writing workshops. She serves as copy editor for the *Northern Appalachia Review* and is a director of the Writing Conference of

Northern Appalachia. Wilson enjoys painting and writing from her home in Moon Township, Pennsylvania, where she resides with her husband, son, dog, and cat. She is currently writing her second book, a novel.

D. D. WOOD is a university supervisor for California State University, Los Angeles and a Master of Arts in Education professor and subject matter expert at Concordia University Irvine. She is currently preparing to defend her dissertation for her Organizational Leadership Ed.D on the relationship between workplace burnout and menopause. She is one of Dani Shapiro's Wishingstone Writers. D. D. is published in *The Chiron Review, Locomotive, The Silver Birch Press, Panorama, The Feminist Anthology, We Were Going to Change the World*, and *Bukowski on Wry*. She is an ageism advocate in arts, media, entertainment, and education and a proud believer in the power of the Crone: the magical, wise woman of mythology.

JUDITH YARROW has been published in, among others, *Women's Words, Cicada, Bellowing Ark, Backbone, Aji, The Bluebird Word*, and *Lit202*. She was the featured poet in *Edge: An International Journal*. Her poems have been included in the Washington State Poet Laureate's 2014 and 2017 collections. She lives in Seattle, Washington, where she gardens, walks, and believes kindness is crucial in all cases.

About the Editors

JULIE ARTMAN, MFA, MLIS, is a librarian at Chapman University and a book reviewer for Association of College and Research Libraries *Choice*. Her co-authored book *Your Craft as a Teaching Librarian: Using Acting Skills to Create a Dynamic Presence* was published in 2022.

STACY RUSSO, MA, MLIS, librarian and associate professor at Santa Ana College, is committed to creating books and art for a more peaceful world. She is a current PhD student at California Institute of Integral Studies. Her dissertation is a study of the autobiographical writings of women who create solo-homes or homes of their own outside of the dominant marriage-and-family paradigm. She is the author of several nonfiction books, the editor of two essay collections, a published poet, and the author/illustrator of two children's picture books. *One Day I Started a New Life*, an art book featuring Stacy's collages and mixed media work over the last decade, is forthcoming from Sacramento-based Litwin Books. Stacy's books have been featured on National Public Radio, Pacifica Radio, the Canadian Broadcasting System, Sirius XM Radio, KCET *Artbound*, *LA Weekly*, and various other media channels. She served as a longtime book reviewer for *Library Journal* and has over seventy published reviews, primarily in the areas of women's literature, American literature, and literary biography. After years of working as a writer within the traditional publishing model, she created Wild Librarian Press in 2021 to independently publish her writing and the work of other writers.